MILITARY CHAPLAINCY

The Role of the Military Chaplain

Dr. Maxwell Shimba

Shimba Publishing, LLC.

Printed in the United States of America

TABLE OF CONTENTS

INTRODUCTION

The Call to Serve

The role of the military chaplain is one steeped in history and tradition, a vocation that blends spiritual guidance with the rigors of military life. From the battlefields of ancient civilizations to the modern theaters of war, military chaplains have stood alongside soldiers, offering solace, wisdom, and spiritual support. This book delves into the life and work of military chaplains, exploring their vital contributions to the emotional and spiritual well-being of soldiers.

In the heat of battle and the quiet moments of reflection that follow, chaplains are there, providing a steady presence and a compassionate ear. They perform religious services, offer counseling, and provide a moral compass for those navigating the moral complexities of warfare. Whether on the front lines or in garrison, chaplains are entrusted with the sacred duty of caring for the soul amidst the chaos of conflict.

The military chaplaincy's origins can be traced back to the earliest days of organized armies, where priests and spiritual advisors accompanied soldiers into battle. These early chaplains were tasked not only with conducting religious rites but also with maintaining the morale and ethical standards of the troops. Over the centuries, the role has evolved, adapting to the changing nature of warfare and the diverse spiritual needs of modern military personnel.

Today's military chaplains are trained to serve in a wide variety of contexts, from the bustling bases of home countries to the remote outposts of conflict zones. They are equipped to minister to soldiers of all faiths and none, embodying a spirit of inclusivity and respect for diverse beliefs. This commitment to serving all service members, regardless of their religious affiliation, is a hallmark of modern military chaplaincy.

The chaplain's role extends beyond the battlefield. In times of peace, they support military families, assist in community outreach, and contribute to the overall resilience and well-being of the military community. Their work is integral to the holistic health of the armed forces, addressing the spiritual, emotional, and ethical dimensions of military life.

This book will explore the multifaceted role of military chaplains through various lenses. We will look at the historical development of the chaplaincy, the daily responsibilities and challenges faced by chaplains, and the profound impact they have on the lives of soldiers. Through case studies, personal testimonials, and in-depth analysis, we aim to shed light on this essential but often overlooked aspect of military service.

At its core, military chaplaincy is about answering a call to serve—a call that demands courage, compassion, and an unwavering commitment to the well-being of others. As we journey through the chapters of this book, we will gain a deeper understanding of what it means to be a military chaplain and the invaluable role they play in supporting those who serve.

This book is a tribute to the men and women who have answered this call, dedicating their lives to the spiritual care of soldiers. It is also an invitation to readers to reflect on the importance of faith, hope, and compassion in the midst of conflict. Through their stories and experiences, we will see how military chaplains embody the highest ideals of service, providing a beacon of light in the darkest of times.

Historical Background of Military Chaplaincy

Tracing back to ancient armies, the presence of spiritual advisors in the military has been documented throughout history. These early chaplains provided not only religious services but also moral support and counsel to warriors facing the uncertainties of battle. From the armies of ancient Rome and Greece to the medieval knights and beyond, the role of the chaplain has been an enduring element of military tradition.

In ancient Rome, spiritual advisors known as "augurs" and "pontiffs" played crucial roles in military campaigns. They conducted religious rituals and interpreted omens to ensure the favor of the gods. These advisors were integral to maintaining the morale and spiritual well-being of Roman soldiers, offering guidance and reassurance in times of conflict.

Similarly, in ancient Greece, priests and oracles were often consulted before and during military campaigns. The famous Oracle of Delphi, for instance, was sought for divine insight and blessings before battles. Greek armies carried sacred objects into battle, believing these would protect them and ensure victory. The presence of these spiritual advisors provided a sense of divine support and legitimacy to their military endeavors.

The role of chaplains continued to evolve during the Middle Ages. Christian priests accompanied medieval knights on their crusades, offering religious services, hearing confessions, and providing last rites. These chaplains were not only spiritual guides but also moral anchors, helping to uphold the ethical codes of chivalry and honor that governed knightly conduct. Their presence was a reminder of the sacred vows and duties that knights were sworn to uphold.

As European armies became more organized in the Renaissance and early modern periods, the role of the military chaplain became more formalized. In the 16th century, the Spanish and Portuguese empires appointed chaplains to accompany their conquistadors and explorers. These chaplains were tasked with converting indigenous populations to Christianity, often under challenging and hostile conditions. Their dual role as spiritual leaders and agents of colonial expansion highlighted the complex and sometimes controversial nature of military chaplaincy.

The Reformation and subsequent religious conflicts of the 17th century further shaped the role of military chaplains. Protestant and Catholic chaplains served their respective armies during the Thirty Years' War, one of Europe's most devastating conflicts. These chaplains provided not only spiritual care but also a sense of religious identity and purpose to the soldiers they served. Their work was instrumental in maintaining the morale and cohesion of armies divided by deep theological differences.

In the American Revolutionary War, chaplains played a significant role in supporting the Continental Army. George Washington recognized the importance of spiritual support and insisted on the appointment of chaplains for each regiment. These chaplains conducted worship services, provided counseling, and boosted the morale of troops fighting for independence. The presence of chaplains underscored the idea that the struggle for liberty was not only a political endeavor but also a deeply moral and spiritual one.

The Civil War in the United States saw an unprecedented number of chaplains serving both the Union and Confederate armies. These chaplains faced immense challenges, ministering to soldiers in the midst of brutal and prolonged conflict. They provided comfort to the wounded and dying, conducted burials, and supported soldiers grappling with the horrors of war. The work of Civil War chaplains highlighted the critical role of spiritual care in maintaining the mental and emotional resilience of soldiers.

In the 20th century, the world wars brought further evolution to the role of military chaplains. During World War I, chaplains served in the trenches, enduring the same hardships as the soldiers they ministered to. They offered prayers, conducted services, and provided much-needed moral support in the face of unprecedented carnage. The chaplains' presence in the trenches symbolized hope and humanity amid the devastation of modern warfare.

World War II saw chaplains serving in even greater numbers and in more diverse capacities. They accompanied troops in every theater of the war, from the deserts of North Africa to the islands of the Pacific. Chaplains provided spiritual care to soldiers of all faiths, reflecting the increasingly pluralistic nature of modern armies. Their work was crucial in maintaining the morale and spiritual resilience of soldiers facing prolonged and grueling campaigns.

The Korean War, the Vietnam War, and subsequent conflicts in the Middle East have continued to highlight the vital role of military chaplains. In each of these conflicts, chaplains have adapted to new challenges, providing spiritual support in increasingly complex and technologically advanced combat environments. They have also played key roles in peacekeeping missions and humanitarian efforts, reflecting the expanding scope of military operations in the modern era.

Throughout history, military chaplains have been more than just religious functionaries. They have been sources of comfort, moral guidance, and resilience for soldiers facing the uncertainties and horrors of war. Their enduring presence in military history underscores the fundamental human need for spiritual support, especially in times of conflict. As we explore the evolving role of military chaplains in this book, we will see how their work continues to be a vital component of military life, providing a beacon of faith and hope in the trenches of battle.

The Evolution of the Role

From its inception to the modern era, the role of the military chaplain has evolved significantly. This evolution mirrors broader changes in military culture and society's understanding of the importance of mental and spiritual health. Today, chaplains serve in various capacities, from conducting religious services in the field to offering confidential counseling and moral guidance, embodying a holistic approach to supporting soldiers.

In the early days of military chaplaincy, the primary focus was on conducting religious rituals and maintaining the moral fabric of the troops. Chaplains were often seen as extensions of their religious institutions, bringing the sacred into the secular world of the military. Their presence was crucial in providing a sense of divine support and legitimacy to military campaigns. However, as the nature of warfare and society's views on religion and spirituality have changed, so too has the role of the chaplain.

During the world wars of the 20th century, the role of chaplains expanded significantly. They were no longer confined to conducting religious services but became integral to the overall well-being of soldiers. Chaplains in World War I and World War II served on the front lines, offering comfort and solace to soldiers in the trenches. They ministered to the wounded, conducted burials, and provided a critical moral presence amidst the chaos of battle. The sheer scale and brutality of these wars underscored the need for a broader approach to chaplaincy, one that addressed not only spiritual needs but also emotional and psychological support.

The post-World War II era saw further changes as chaplains began to receive specialized training to deal with the diverse challenges of modern military life. This period marked the beginning of a more professionalized chaplaincy, with chaplains being trained in pastoral care, counseling, and ethics. The recognition of post-traumatic stress disorder (PTSD) and other psychological impacts of combat highlighted the importance of mental health care, and chaplains became key players in addressing these issues.

In the Korean and Vietnam Wars, chaplains continued to adapt to new realities. The unconventional nature of these conflicts, with their guerrilla warfare and complex political dimensions, required chaplains to be more versatile and resilient. They provided not only spiritual support but also a listening ear and a source of stability for soldiers facing prolonged and ambiguous combat situations. The Vietnam War, in particular, brought to light the moral and ethical dilemmas faced by soldiers, and chaplains played a crucial role in helping them navigate these challenges.

The end of the Cold War and the emergence of new types of conflicts, such as peacekeeping missions and counter-insurgency operations, further expanded the role of chaplains. They became involved in humanitarian efforts, working alongside military personnel to provide aid and support to civilian populations affected by conflict. This period also saw an increasing recognition of the need for chaplains to be culturally sensitive and adept at working in diverse environments.

In the 21st century, the role of military chaplains has continued to evolve in response to the changing nature of warfare and the growing recognition of the importance of mental and spiritual health. In conflicts such as those in Iraq and Afghanistan, chaplains have served in a variety of capacities, from providing spiritual care in remote forward operating bases to supporting families on the home front. They have also been involved in addressing the complex issues of moral injury, where soldiers struggle with actions that conflict with their moral and ethical beliefs.

Today's military chaplains are trained to be versatile and adaptable, equipped to handle a wide range of issues. They provide confidential counseling, helping soldiers cope with the stresses of military life and the impacts of combat.

They offer moral guidance, assisting soldiers in navigating ethical dilemmas and making decisions that align with their values. Chaplains also conduct religious services and ceremonies, providing opportunities for soldiers to practice their faith and find spiritual nourishment.

The modern chaplaincy reflects a holistic approach to soldier care, recognizing that spiritual health is interconnected with mental and emotional well-being. Chaplains work closely with mental health professionals, medical staff, and commanders to ensure that soldiers receive comprehensive support. This collaborative approach underscores the importance of addressing the full spectrum of a soldier's needs, from physical health to spiritual resilience.

Furthermore, the diversity of today's military has prompted chaplains to be more inclusive and respectful of different faiths and beliefs. Chaplains are trained to provide spiritual support to soldiers of all religious backgrounds, as well as to those who do not identify with any faith. This inclusivity is essential in fostering a sense of belonging and respect within the military community.

The evolution of the military chaplain's role also reflects broader societal changes in the understanding of mental and spiritual health. There is a growing recognition of the importance of addressing the psychological and emotional impacts of combat, and chaplains are at the forefront of these efforts. Their work is crucial in promoting resilience, fostering a sense of purpose, and helping soldiers find meaning in their experiences.

In conclusion, the role of the military chaplain has evolved from a primarily religious function to a multifaceted and holistic approach to soldier care. Today's chaplains are trained to address a wide range of spiritual, emotional, and ethical needs, reflecting the changing nature of warfare and society's understanding of mental and spiritual health. As we continue to explore the lives and work of military chaplains in this book, we will see how their enduring commitment to serving those who serve remains a vital component of military life.

DR. MAXWELL SHIMBA

CHAPTER 01

THE FOUNDATIONS OF MILITARY CHAPLAINCY

Origins and Early History

The concept of military chaplaincy is as old as warfare itself. From the earliest days of organized conflict, armies have recognized the need for spiritual guidance and moral support. Ancient armies often included priests and spiritual advisors who provided not only religious services but also moral and ethical guidance to warriors. These early chaplains played a crucial role in maintaining the morale and spiritual well-being of soldiers, ensuring that they remained steadfast and resolute in the face of the uncertainties and horrors of battle.

In ancient Rome, spiritual advisors known as augurs and pontiffs were integral to military operations. These religious figures performed rituals to interpret the will of the gods, seeking divine favor and guidance before and during military campaigns. The presence of augurs and pontiffs provided soldiers with a sense of security and divine support, reinforcing their belief in the righteousness of their cause and their likelihood of success.

Similarly, ancient Greek armies often sought the counsel of oracles and priests before embarking on military ventures. The Oracle of Delphi, one of the most famous religious sites in ancient Greece, was frequently consulted by military leaders. Soldiers believed that the gods' favor was essential for victory, and the guidance provided by these spiritual advisors was seen as a crucial element of military strategy.

The role of spiritual advisors continued to evolve during the medieval period. Christian priests accompanied European knights on their crusades, providing religious services, hearing confessions, and offering last rites to the dying. These chaplains were not only spiritual guides but also moral anchors, helping to uphold the ethical codes of chivalry and honor that governed knightly conduct. Their presence was a constant reminder of the sacred vows and duties that knights were sworn to uphold, imbuing their military endeavors with a sense of divine mission and purpose.

As European armies became more organized and professionalized during the Renaissance and early modern periods, the role of the chaplain became more formalized. In the 16th century, the Spanish and Portuguese empires appointed chaplains to accompany their conquistadors and explorers. These chaplains were tasked with converting indigenous populations to Christianity, often under challenging and hostile conditions. Their dual role as spiritual leaders and agents of colonial expansion highlighted the complex and sometimes controversial nature of military chaplaincy.

The Reformation and subsequent religious conflicts of the 17th century further shaped the role of military chaplains. Protestant and Catholic chaplains served their respective armies during the Thirty Years' War, one of Europe's most devastating conflicts. These chaplains provided not only spiritual care but also a sense of religious identity and purpose to the soldiers they served. Their work was instrumental in maintaining the morale and cohesion of armies divided by deep theological differences.

In the American Revolutionary War, chaplains played a significant role in supporting the Continental Army. George Washington recognized the importance of spiritual support and insisted on the appointment of chaplains for each regiment. These chaplains conducted worship services, provided counseling, and boosted the morale of troops fighting for independence. The presence of chaplains underscored the idea that the struggle for liberty was not only a political endeavor but also a deeply moral and spiritual one.

The Civil War in the United States saw an unprecedented number of chaplains serving both the Union and Confederate armies. These chaplains faced immense challenges, ministering to soldiers in the midst of brutal and prolonged conflict. They provided comfort to the wounded and dying, conducted burials, and supported soldiers grappling with the horrors of war. The work of Civil War chaplains highlighted the critical role of spiritual care in maintaining the mental and emotional resilience of soldiers.

In the 20th century, the world wars brought further evolution to the role of military chaplains. During World War I, chaplains served in the trenches, enduring the same hardships as the soldiers they ministered to. They offered prayers, conducted services, and provided much-needed moral support in the face of unprecedented carnage. The chaplains' presence in the trenches symbolized hope and humanity amid the devastation of modern warfare.

World War II saw chaplains serving in even greater numbers and in more diverse capacities. They accompanied troops in every theater of the war, from the deserts of North Africa to the islands of the Pacific. Chaplains provided spiritual care to soldiers of all faiths, reflecting the increasingly pluralistic nature of modern armies. Their work was crucial in maintaining the morale and spiritual resilience of soldiers facing prolonged and grueling campaigns.

The Korean War, the Vietnam War, and subsequent conflicts in the Middle East have continued to highlight the vital role of military chaplains. In each of these conflicts, chaplains have adapted to new challenges, providing spiritual support in increasingly complex and technologically advanced combat environments. They have also played key roles in peacekeeping missions and humanitarian efforts, reflecting the expanding scope of military operations in the modern era.

Throughout history, military chaplains have been more than just religious functionaries. They have been sources of comfort, moral guidance, and resilience for soldiers facing the uncertainties and horrors of war. Their enduring presence in military history underscores the fundamental human need for spiritual support, especially in times of conflict. As we explore the evolving role of military chaplains in this book, we will see how their work continues to be a vital component of military life, providing a beacon of faith and hope in the trenches of battle.

Key Figures and Milestones

Throughout history, there have been numerous notable figures who have shaped the development of military chaplaincy. These individuals have left an indelible mark on the field, influencing the ways in which spiritual guidance and military service intersect. Their lives and work have set precedents and provided frameworks that continue to guide military chaplains today.

One of the earliest and most influential figures in the history of military chaplaincy is St. Martin of Tours. Born in 316 AD in what is now Hungary, Martin was the son of a Roman soldier and followed in his father's footsteps by joining the Roman army. However, Martin's life took a dramatic turn when he encountered Christianity. Despite his military career, he was drawn to the teachings of Christ and was baptized at the age of 18.

The most famous story about Martin's life occurred while he was still a soldier. According to legend, Martin encountered a beggar shivering in the cold. Moved by compassion, Martin cut his military cloak in half and shared it with the beggar. That night, he had a vision of Christ wearing the half-cloak and saying, "Martin, who is still but a catechumen, has clothed me with this garment." This experience solidified Martin's faith and led him to pursue a life of religious devotion.

After leaving the military, Martin became a monk and eventually was appointed Bishop of Tours in France. As bishop, Martin continued to embody the integration of faith and service, working tirelessly to spread Christianity and care for the poor and oppressed. His life and work set a powerful example of how military service and Christian faith could coexist, and he is often considered the patron saint of soldiers.

Another key figure in the history of military chaplaincy is George Fox, the founder of the Religious Society of Friends, commonly known as the Quakers. Born in 1624 in England, Fox experienced a deep spiritual awakening in his early twenties. He became a fervent preacher, emphasizing direct, personal experiences of God over formal religious rituals and doctrines.

Fox's teachings on pacifism and moral integrity had a profound impact on his followers, many of whom faced persecution for their beliefs. During the English Civil War, Fox and the early Quakers took a bold stand against violence, refusing to bear arms or participate in military activities. Instead, they emphasized the importance of moral guidance and the pursuit of peace.

Although Fox himself did not serve as a military chaplain, his influence extended to those who did. Quaker principles of nonviolence and ethical conduct have shaped the approach of many military chaplains, particularly in times of conflict. The emphasis on providing moral guidance and supporting soldiers in making ethical decisions resonates deeply with Fox's teachings.

In the American Revolutionary War, another significant figure emerged: George Washington, the commander-in-chief of the Continental Army. Recognizing the importance of spiritual support for his troops, Washington insisted on the appointment of chaplains for each regiment. He understood that faith could provide soldiers with the strength and resilience needed to endure the hardships of war.

Washington's leadership set a precedent for the inclusion of chaplains in the American military. His commitment to ensuring that soldiers had access to spiritual care underscored the belief that military service and faith were not mutually exclusive but could be complementary. The Continental Army's chaplains played a crucial role in maintaining morale and providing comfort during the Revolutionary War.

During the American Civil War, both Union and Confederate armies relied heavily on chaplains to support their troops. One notable chaplain from this period was Father William Corby, a Catholic priest who served with the Irish Brigade of the Union Army. On the eve of the Battle of Gettysburg, Father Corby stood on a rock and gave a general absolution to the soldiers, offering them spiritual solace before one of the bloodiest battles of the war.

Father Corby's actions were a poignant reminder of the chaplain's role in providing spiritual support and comfort in times of extreme stress and danger. His presence at Gettysburg became an iconic symbol of the chaplain's duty to care for the souls of soldiers, regardless of the circumstances.

In the 20th century, World War I and World War II saw the emergence of several influential chaplains who left lasting legacies. One such figure was Chaplain Emil Kapaun, a Catholic priest who served in both World War II and the Korean War. Known for his bravery and selflessness, Kapaun ministered to soldiers on the front lines, often risking his life to provide comfort and support.

During the Korean War, Kapaun was captured by enemy forces and endured harsh conditions as a prisoner of war. Despite the dire circumstances, he continued to serve his fellow prisoners, providing spiritual guidance and physical care. His unwavering dedication earned him the Medal of Honor posthumously, and he is remembered as a model of courage and compassion.

Another notable chaplain from World War II was Rabbi Alexander Goode, one of the "Four Chaplains" who sacrificed their lives during the sinking of the USS Dorchester in 1943. Alongside a Catholic priest, a Protestant minister, and a Dutch Reformed chaplain, Rabbi Goode gave up his life jacket to save others and provided spiritual comfort as the ship went down. The story of the Four Chaplains is a powerful testament to the chaplain's commitment to selfless service and interfaith solidarity.

In more recent conflicts, chaplains like Chaplain Barry C. Black, the first African American to serve as the Chief of Chaplains of the United States Navy, have continued to shape the field. Appointed in 2000, Chaplain Black has emphasized the importance of diversity and inclusion within the chaplaincy, reflecting the evolving nature of the military and society as a whole.

These key figures and milestones illustrate the rich and diverse history of military chaplaincy. From St. Martin of Tours to modern-day chaplains, the role has been shaped by individuals who have dedicated their lives to serving both God and country. Their contributions have ensured that soldiers receive the spiritual care and moral guidance needed to navigate the challenges of military life, providing a lasting legacy of faith and service.

Chaplaincy in Different Military Branches

Each branch of the military has its own unique approach to chaplaincy, reflecting its distinct culture, mission, and operational environment. This section explores the distinct roles and responsibilities of chaplains in the Army, Navy, Air Force, and Marine Corps, highlighting how each branch addresses the spiritual needs of its members.

Army Chaplaincy

The Army is the largest branch of the U.S. military, and its chaplaincy is correspondingly extensive and varied. Army chaplains are embedded within units at all levels, from battalion to division, providing spiritual support directly to soldiers wherever they are deployed. They conduct religious services, offer pastoral counseling, and provide moral guidance, helping soldiers cope with the stresses of military life and the challenges of combat.

Army chaplains are also involved in humanitarian missions, peacekeeping operations, and disaster response efforts. They often serve in remote and austere environments, requiring adaptability and resilience. The Army places a strong emphasis on the integration of chaplains into the daily lives of soldiers, ensuring that spiritual care is always accessible.

One of the unique aspects of Army chaplaincy is its focus on unit cohesion and morale. Chaplains play a critical role in building and maintaining the esprit de corps of their units, fostering a sense of community and mutual support. They are trusted advisors to commanders, providing insights into the moral and ethical dimensions of leadership and decision-making.

Navy Chaplaincy

Navy chaplains serve a diverse and dispersed community, including sailors on ships, submarines, and bases around the world. The Navy's global reach and maritime environment present unique challenges and opportunities for chaplains, who must be prepared to minister in a variety of settings, from the deck of an aircraft carrier to an isolated duty station.

Navy chaplains are responsible for the spiritual well-being of not only sailors but also Marines and Coast Guardsmen, reflecting the Navy's close operational relationships with these branches. They provide religious services, counseling, and support to personnel and their families, addressing the specific challenges of life at sea and long deployments.

A distinctive feature of Navy chaplaincy is the emphasis on interfaith cooperation and inclusivity. Given the confined and diverse nature of shipboard life, chaplains must be skilled in ministering to individuals of different faiths and beliefs, fostering an environment of mutual respect and understanding. They often serve as mediators and facilitators, helping to maintain harmony and morale within the close-knit shipboard community.

Air Force Chaplaincy

Air Force chaplains serve in a branch known for its technological prowess and strategic missions. The Air Force's focus on air and space superiority requires chaplains to be adaptable and innovative, providing spiritual care to personnel involved in complex and often high-stress operations.

Air Force chaplains are stationed at bases around the world, where they conduct religious services, offer pastoral counseling, and provide ethical guidance. They support airmen and their families, addressing the unique challenges of frequent relocations, long deployments, and high-tempo operations. The Air Force chaplaincy also places a strong emphasis on resilience and mental health, working closely with medical and mental health professionals to support the overall well-being of airmen.

One of the distinctive aspects of Air Force chaplaincy is its focus on the integration of faith and technology. Chaplains use digital tools and platforms to reach airmen deployed in remote locations, providing virtual counseling and support. This innovative approach ensures that spiritual care is accessible even in the most challenging and technologically advanced environments.

Marine Corps Chaplaincy

Marine Corps chaplains serve a branch known for its rigorous physical and mental demands, as well as its strong sense of tradition and camaraderie. The Marine Corps' ethos of "Semper Fidelis" (Always Faithful) is reflected in the dedication and resilience of its chaplains, who provide spiritual support to Marines in some of the most demanding environments.

Marine Corps chaplains are embedded within Marine units, often deploying alongside them to combat zones and austere environments. They conduct religious services, offer counseling, and provide moral guidance, helping Marines cope with the stresses of combat and the challenges of military life. The close-knit and highly disciplined nature of Marine units requires chaplains to be highly adaptable and resilient, capable of providing support under extreme conditions.

A unique aspect of Marine Corps chaplaincy is the emphasis on character development and ethical leadership. Chaplains play a key role in instilling the core values of honor, courage, and commitment, working closely with commanders to foster a culture of integrity and ethical behavior. They also support Marines' families, providing resources and counseling to help them navigate the challenges of military life.

Conclusion

Each branch of the military has its own unique approach to chaplaincy, reflecting its distinct culture, mission, and operational environment. Army chaplains focus on unit cohesion and morale, Navy chaplains emphasize interfaith cooperation and inclusivity, Air Force chaplains integrate faith and technology, and Marine Corps chaplains highlight character development and ethical leadership. Despite these differences, all military chaplains share a common commitment to providing spiritual support and moral guidance to service members, ensuring that they have the resources and resilience needed to fulfill their duties. The diversity of chaplaincy across the branches underscores the adaptability and dedication of chaplains in serving those who serve.

CHAPTER 02

THE CHAPLAIN'S ROLE IN MODERN WARFARE

Daily Duties and Responsibilities

Modern military chaplains are tasked with a wide range of duties, reflecting the complex and multifaceted nature of their role. They are spiritual leaders, counselors, ethical advisors, and confidants, providing a constant source of support and stability for soldiers in various stages of deployment. Their daily responsibilities are diverse and demanding, requiring adaptability, resilience, and a deep commitment to service.

Conducting Worship Services and Administering Sacraments

One of the primary duties of military chaplains is to conduct worship services and administer sacraments. These religious ceremonies provide soldiers with the opportunity to practice their faith, find spiritual solace, and build a sense of community. Whether in a chapel on a military base, in a makeshift shelter in the field, or aboard a ship, chaplains ensure that soldiers have access to regular worship and the sacraments of their faith.

Chaplains lead services for various religious denominations, reflecting the diversity of faiths within the military. They conduct Christian services, Jewish prayers, Muslim salat, and other religious observances, adapting to the needs of the soldiers they serve. This inclusivity fosters an environment of mutual respect and understanding, allowing soldiers of different faiths to coexist harmoniously.

Providing Pastoral Care and Counseling

Pastoral care and counseling are central to the chaplain's role. Military life can be stressful and challenging, with soldiers facing physical danger, emotional strain, and the pressures of long deployments away from family and friends. Chaplains provide a compassionate and non-judgmental ear, offering confidential counseling to help soldiers navigate these challenges.

Chaplains address a wide range of issues, including relationship problems, stress and anxiety, grief and loss, and moral and ethical dilemmas. They provide crisis intervention, helping soldiers cope with traumatic experiences and mental health issues such as post-traumatic stress disorder (PTSD). Through one-on-one counseling sessions, group therapy, and support groups, chaplains help soldiers build resilience and find hope in difficult times.

Ethical Guidance and Moral Leadership

Chaplains serve as ethical advisors and moral leaders within the military. They provide guidance on ethical issues and dilemmas, helping soldiers and commanders make decisions that align with their values and the ethical standards of their profession. This role is particularly important in the context of modern warfare, where soldiers may face complex moral challenges and the pressures of rapid decision-making in high-stakes environments.

Chaplains offer training and education on ethical leadership, character development, and moral reasoning. They facilitate discussions on topics such as the rules of engagement, the treatment of non-combatants, and the principles of just war theory. By fostering a culture of integrity and ethical behavior, chaplains contribute to the overall moral resilience of the military.

Supporting Families and Building Community

The chaplain's role extends beyond the individual soldier to include support for military families and the broader community. Military life often involves frequent relocations, long separations, and the challenges of raising a family in a high-pressure environment. Chaplains provide resources, counseling, and support to help families navigate these challenges and build strong, resilient relationships.

Chaplains organize family support programs, marriage retreats, and parenting workshops, creating opportunities for families to connect and support one another. They also offer counseling and support for children, helping them cope with the unique challenges of growing up in a military family. By fostering a sense of community and belonging, chaplains help families thrive in the demanding context of military life.

Crisis Response and Humanitarian Aid

In times of crisis, chaplains play a vital role in providing support and humanitarian aid. Whether responding to natural disasters, accidents, or acts of violence, chaplains offer spiritual care, comfort, and practical assistance to those affected. They work alongside medical and emergency response teams, providing emotional and spiritual support to victims and their families.

Chaplains also participate in humanitarian missions, both domestically and internationally. They provide aid and support to communities affected by conflict, poverty, and natural disasters, embodying the values of compassion and service. These efforts not only address immediate needs but also build goodwill and strengthen relationships between the military and the communities they serve.

Promoting Resilience and Well-Being

A key aspect of the chaplain's role is promoting resilience and overall well-being among soldiers. Chaplains work to enhance the spiritual, emotional, and mental health of soldiers through a variety of programs and initiatives. They lead workshops on stress management, mindfulness, and spiritual resilience, helping soldiers develop the skills and practices needed to thrive in challenging environments.

Chaplains also collaborate with mental health professionals, medical staff, and commanders to ensure a holistic approach to soldier care. They advocate for the well-being of soldiers, identifying and addressing issues that may impact their readiness and resilience. By fostering a culture of care and support, chaplains contribute to the overall effectiveness and morale of the military.

Interfaith and Multicultural Engagement

Modern military chaplains must be adept at navigating the diverse and multicultural landscape of today's armed forces. They engage with soldiers of various religious backgrounds and beliefs, providing inclusive spiritual support and fostering an environment of respect and understanding.

This interfaith engagement is essential in promoting unity and cohesion within a diverse military community.

Chaplains facilitate interfaith dialogues, organize multicultural events, and work to ensure that the religious needs of all soldiers are met. They serve as advocates for religious freedom and accommodation, helping soldiers practice their faith while fulfilling their military duties. This commitment to inclusivity strengthens the bonds of trust and solidarity within the military.

Adapting to Technological and Operational Changes

The modern military is characterized by rapid technological advancements and evolving operational environments. Chaplains must adapt to these changes, using technology to extend their reach and provide support in new and innovative ways. From virtual counseling sessions to online worship services, chaplains leverage digital tools to connect with soldiers, regardless of their location.

Chaplains also stay abreast of changes in military operations, ensuring that they can effectively support soldiers in diverse and often challenging environments. Whether serving on the front lines, aboard ships, or in remote outposts, chaplains remain committed to their mission of providing spiritual care and moral guidance.

Conclusion

The daily duties and responsibilities of modern military chaplains are diverse and demanding, reflecting the complex nature of their role. From conducting worship services and administering sacraments to providing pastoral care, ethical guidance, and crisis response, chaplains are a constant source of support and stability for soldiers. Their work is essential in promoting the spiritual, emotional, and mental well-being of military personnel, ensuring that they are equipped to face the challenges of modern warfare. As we continue to explore the role of chaplains in this book, we will gain a deeper appreciation for their vital contributions to the military and the lives of those they serve.

Providing Spiritual Guidance and Support

One of the core responsibilities of military chaplains is to offer spiritual guidance and support tailored to the diverse religious beliefs represented in the military. In the melting pot of modern armed forces, where soldiers come from various cultural and religious backgrounds, chaplains play a crucial role in ensuring that each individual's spiritual needs are met. This involves leading prayers, facilitating religious study groups, and offering personalized one-on-one counseling sessions.

Leading Prayers and Worship Services

Chaplains lead prayers and conduct worship services that cater to the religious practices of their unit members. Whether in a chapel, a makeshift tent, or an open field, these services provide soldiers with an opportunity to practice their faith and find solace in their beliefs. For Christian soldiers, this might include Sunday services, Eucharist, or confession. For Jewish soldiers, chaplains might lead Shabbat services and observances of Jewish holidays. Muslim soldiers might rely on chaplains to help facilitate Jumu'ah prayers on Fridays and observe Ramadan.

The inclusivity of chaplain-led services is a hallmark of their approach. Chaplains often work with lay leaders from various faith groups to ensure that all soldiers, regardless of their religion, have access to spiritual support. This collaboration helps build a sense of community and mutual respect among soldiers of different faiths.

Facilitating Religious Study Groups

Beyond leading formal services, chaplains facilitate religious study groups that allow soldiers to deepen their understanding of their faith and engage in meaningful discussions. These study groups might take the form of Bible studies, Torah studies, Quranic studies, or discussions on Buddhist teachings, depending on the needs of the soldiers.

Religious study groups provide a platform for soldiers to ask questions, share their thoughts, and support one another in their spiritual journeys. These sessions often foster a sense of camaraderie and mutual support, helping soldiers build strong, faith-based relationships that can be a source of strength and encouragement in challenging times.

Offering One-on-One Counseling Sessions

One-on-one counseling sessions are a vital component of the chaplain's role in providing spiritual guidance and support. These confidential sessions offer soldiers a safe space to discuss their spiritual concerns, seek advice, and receive personalized support. Chaplains listen with empathy and provide guidance rooted in their religious and ethical training, helping soldiers navigate personal and spiritual challenges.

These counseling sessions address a wide range of issues, including doubts about faith, moral dilemmas, grief and loss, and the search for meaning and purpose. Chaplains help soldiers reconcile their experiences and emotions with their spiritual beliefs, providing a sense of direction and hope.

For many soldiers, these one-on-one sessions are a lifeline, offering them the opportunity to explore their spirituality in depth and find peace amidst the turmoil of military life. The trust and confidentiality inherent in the chaplain-soldier relationship are critical in fostering open and honest communication.

Support for Religious Observances

Chaplains also play a key role in supporting soldiers' religious observances, ensuring that they can practice their faith even in the challenging conditions of military life. This includes facilitating access to religious materials, arranging for special services during significant religious holidays, and advocating for accommodations that allow soldiers to observe religious practices.

For example, during Ramadan, chaplains may work to ensure that Muslim soldiers have access to appropriate meals at the end of fasting days and are able to participate in nightly prayers. During Passover, Jewish chaplains may help organize Seder meals and provide kosher food options. For Christian holidays such as Easter and Christmas, chaplains ensure that soldiers can participate in services and celebrations that are meaningful to them.

By supporting these observances, chaplains help soldiers maintain a sense of continuity and connection with their faith, providing a source of comfort and stability.

Fostering Interfaith Understanding

In a military environment characterized by religious diversity, chaplains play a crucial role in fostering interfaith understanding and respect. They facilitate dialogues and educational programs that promote awareness and appreciation of different religious traditions. This interfaith engagement helps build a culture of mutual respect and reduces misunderstandings and conflicts that can arise from religious differences.

Chaplains may organize interfaith services, panel discussions, and cultural events that celebrate the rich tapestry of beliefs within the military community. By creating opportunities for soldiers to learn about and from each other's faiths, chaplains help build a cohesive and inclusive environment.

Navigating Ethical and Moral Challenges

Modern warfare presents soldiers with complex ethical and moral challenges. Chaplains provide essential support in helping soldiers navigate these issues, offering guidance rooted in their faith traditions. Whether dealing with the moral implications of combat, the treatment of non-combatants, or decisions that conflict with personal beliefs, soldiers often turn to chaplains for advice and support.

Chaplains facilitate ethical discussions and provide a moral framework that helps soldiers make decisions aligned with their values and the ethical standards of their profession.

This guidance is crucial in maintaining the integrity and moral resilience of the military.

Conclusion

Providing spiritual guidance and support is a cornerstone of the chaplain's role in modern warfare. Through leading prayers and worship services, facilitating religious study groups, offering one-on-one counseling, supporting religious observances, fostering interfaith understanding, and navigating ethical challenges, chaplains ensure that soldiers have the spiritual resources they need to thrive. Their work is essential in promoting the spiritual well-being of military personnel, fostering a sense of community, and upholding the moral fabric of the military. As we continue to explore the chaplain's role, we will see how their dedication and compassion make a profound difference in the lives of those they serve.

Conducting Religious Services in the Field

Even in the harshest conditions, military chaplains find ways to conduct religious services, ensuring that soldiers can practice their faith regardless of their location. This adaptability is crucial in maintaining the spiritual well-being of troops, providing them with a sense of normalcy and continuity amidst the uncertainties of military life.

Adapting to Challenging Environments

Military chaplains are trained to conduct religious services in a variety of environments, from the relative comfort of a base chapel to the austere conditions of a forward operating base or a naval ship. This flexibility is essential in ensuring that soldiers have access to spiritual support wherever they are deployed.

In combat zones, chaplains often set up makeshift altars using whatever materials are available, transforming a simple tent, an open field, or even the back of a vehicle into a sacred space. These impromptu settings become places of worship where soldiers can gather for prayer, reflection, and community. The ability to adapt to challenging environments is a hallmark of the chaplaincy, reflecting their commitment to serving soldiers under any circumstances.

Multidenominational and Inclusive Services

Given the diverse religious beliefs represented within the military, chaplains frequently conduct multidenominational and inclusive services that cater to the spiritual needs of all soldiers. These services are designed to be respectful and accommodating of various faith traditions, allowing soldiers from different backgrounds to worship together.

For example, a field service might include prayers and readings from multiple religious texts, ensuring that everyone feels included and valued. Chaplains also work with lay leaders and representatives from different faith groups to ensure that specific religious needs are met, fostering a sense of unity and mutual respect among soldiers.

Creative Use of Resources

Conducting religious services in the field often requires creative use of resources. Chaplains may use portable communion kits, travel-sized religious texts, and battery-operated candles to facilitate worship in remote locations. They might also rely on technology, such as audio recordings of hymns or digital prayer books, to enhance the worship experience.

In some cases, chaplains may have to improvise, using everyday items to symbolize religious artifacts. A simple piece of cloth might serve as an altar cloth, a water bottle as a baptismal font, and a metal container as a chalice. These resourceful solutions demonstrate the chaplains' dedication to ensuring that soldiers can practice their faith regardless of logistical challenges.

Timing and Frequency of Services

The timing and frequency of religious services in the field are often dictated by operational demands and the availability of soldiers. Chaplains work closely with unit commanders to schedule services at times that minimize disruption to military operations while maximizing attendance.

Services might be held early in the morning before the day's activities begin, during a lull in operations, or in the evening when soldiers return from their duties. The flexibility of chaplains in accommodating the schedules of their units ensures that as many soldiers as possible can participate in worship and receive spiritual support.

Providing Comfort and Hope

In the harsh and often dangerous conditions of military deployments, religious services conducted by chaplains provide soldiers with comfort and hope. These services offer a sense of peace and stability, allowing soldiers to find solace in their faith and connect with something greater than themselves.

The familiar rituals and prayers of religious services can be profoundly reassuring, reminding soldiers of their spiritual roots and providing a sense of continuity amidst the disruptions of military life. Chaplains often include messages of encouragement and resilience in their sermons, helping soldiers to maintain their morale and focus.

Building Community and Fellowship

Religious services in the field also play a vital role in building community and fellowship among soldiers. These gatherings provide an opportunity for soldiers to come together, share their faith experiences, and support one another. The sense of camaraderie and mutual care fostered during these services strengthens the bonds between soldiers, enhancing unit cohesion and morale.

Chaplains facilitate this sense of community by encouraging participation and interaction during services. Soldiers might be invited to share personal reflections, lead prayers, or read from religious texts. These interactive elements help to create a supportive and inclusive environment where everyone feels valued and connected.

Navigating Religious Diversity

Military chaplains are skilled in navigating the religious diversity of their units, ensuring that all soldiers feel respected and included. They work to create an atmosphere of mutual respect and understanding, where soldiers of different faiths can worship together and support one another.

Chaplains also advocate for the religious rights of soldiers, ensuring that their needs are met and that they can practice their faith freely. This might involve coordinating with higher command to provide access to religious materials, arranging for dietary accommodations, or facilitating the observance of religious holidays.

Conclusion

Conducting religious services in the field is a vital aspect of the chaplain's role in modern warfare. By adapting to challenging environments, offering multidenominational and inclusive services, using creative resources, and providing comfort and hope, chaplains ensure that soldiers can practice their faith regardless of their location. These services play a crucial role in maintaining the spiritual well-being of troops, building community, and fostering resilience. As we continue to explore the role of chaplains, we will see how their dedication and adaptability make a profound difference in the lives of those they serve.

CHAPTER 03

CHALLENGES FACED BY MILITARY CHAPLAINS

Navigating the Battlefield: Physical and Emotional Strains

Serving alongside soldiers, chaplains face many of the same physical and emotional challenges that their fellow service members encounter. From the dangers of combat to the stress of long deployments and the emotional toll of ministering to those in distress, military chaplains must employ resilience and coping strategies to fulfill their demanding roles. This section examines the multifaceted challenges chaplains face and the methods they use to navigate these difficulties.

Physical Strains of Combat and Deployment

Military chaplains are often embedded within units that operate in the harshest environments and under the most strenuous conditions. They share the physical hardships of deployment, including extreme weather, difficult terrain, and the constant threat of enemy action. Like the soldiers they serve, chaplains must endure long marches, carry heavy equipment, and maintain a high level of physical fitness to keep up with their units.

The physical demands of deployment can take a toll on chaplains, who must remain physically capable while also providing spiritual and emotional support to others. This dual responsibility requires a high level of stamina and resilience, as chaplains are often called upon to minister at any hour, sometimes under fire or in the immediate aftermath of combat.

Emotional Strains and Vicarious Trauma

The emotional strains faced by military chaplains are profound and multifaceted. They provide support to soldiers experiencing fear, grief, and trauma, often absorbing and processing these intense emotions themselves. This vicarious trauma can lead to emotional exhaustion and compassion fatigue, making it challenging for chaplains to maintain their own mental health while caring for others.

Chaplains frequently encounter soldiers who are grappling with the loss of comrades, the moral ambiguities of combat, and the stresses of being far from home and loved ones. They are present during some of the most harrowing moments of a soldier's life, offering comfort and guidance amidst the chaos. The emotional weight of these experiences can be overwhelming, requiring chaplains to develop robust coping mechanisms to manage their own well-being.

Resilience and Coping Strategies

To navigate the physical and emotional strains of their roles, military chaplains employ a variety of resilience and coping strategies. These strategies are essential for maintaining their effectiveness and well-being in the face of ongoing challenges.

1. Self-Care Practices: Chaplains prioritize self-care to maintain their physical, emotional, and spiritual health. This includes regular exercise, healthy eating, adequate rest, and engaging in activities that promote relaxation and mental clarity. By taking care of their own needs, chaplains ensure they are better equipped to care for others.

2. Spiritual Practices: Maintaining their own spiritual well-being is crucial for chaplains. They engage in regular prayer, meditation, and other spiritual practices that provide solace and strength. These practices help chaplains stay

grounded and connected to their faith, which is a vital source of resilience.

3. Peer Support and Supervision: Chaplains often rely on peer support and supervision to process their experiences and receive emotional and professional guidance. Regular meetings with fellow chaplains and supervisors provide a space to discuss challenges, share insights, and receive support. This collegial environment helps chaplains feel less isolated and more understood.

4. Mental Health Resources: Access to mental health resources is essential for chaplains, who may seek counseling or therapy to address their own emotional needs. Professional mental health support can help chaplains manage stress, process trauma, and develop healthy coping mechanisms.

5. Boundaries and Time Management: Setting boundaries and managing their time effectively allows chaplains to balance their responsibilities and avoid burnout. This includes knowing when to take breaks, delegating tasks when possible, and ensuring they have time for rest and recovery.

6. Resilience Training: Many chaplains undergo resilience training that equips them with skills to handle stress and adversity. This training often includes techniques for

stress management, emotional regulation, and maintaining a positive outlook in challenging situations.

7. Reflection and Journaling: Reflecting on their experiences and journaling can help chaplains process their emotions and gain perspective. This practice allows chaplains to articulate their thoughts and feelings, providing a constructive outlet for the emotional strains they encounter.

The Role of Chaplains in Supporting Each Other

In addition to these individual coping strategies, chaplains often support one another through mentorship and camaraderie. Experienced chaplains provide guidance and encouragement to newer chaplains, helping them navigate the complexities of their roles. This mentorship fosters a sense of community and shared purpose, which is invaluable in sustaining morale and resilience.

Chaplains also participate in professional development and continuing education, which provide opportunities to learn new skills, stay informed about best practices, and connect with peers. These programs reinforce the importance of ongoing growth and adaptation in the face of evolving challenges.

Conclusion

Navigating the battlefield's physical and emotional strains is a significant challenge for military chaplains. Their ability to remain resilient and effective in such demanding conditions is a testament to their dedication and the robust coping strategies they employ. By prioritizing self-care, maintaining their spiritual practices, seeking support, and continually developing their skills, chaplains ensure they can provide the essential spiritual and emotional support that soldiers need. As we continue to explore the challenges faced by military chaplains, we will gain a deeper appreciation for their resilience and the vital role they play in the lives of those they serve.

Addressing Diverse Faiths and Beliefs

In a pluralistic military environment, chaplains must navigate and respect a wide array of religious beliefs and practices. This requires a deep understanding of different faiths and an ability to provide inclusive spiritual support that honors the diverse backgrounds of the soldiers they serve. The modern military is a microcosm of society, reflecting its rich tapestry of cultures, religions, and worldviews. For chaplains, this diversity presents both challenges and opportunities.

Understanding Different Faiths

To effectively serve a diverse military population, chaplains must have a broad and nuanced understanding of various religious traditions. This includes knowledge of major world religions such as Christianity, Islam, Judaism, Hinduism, and Buddhism, as well as an awareness of less widely practiced faiths and spiritual beliefs. Chaplains receive training in world religions, allowing them to appreciate the unique aspects of each faith and to provide appropriate spiritual care.

Understanding different faiths goes beyond academic knowledge; it requires empathy and a willingness to engage with soldiers' beliefs on a personal level. Chaplains often participate in interfaith dialogues and cultural exchange programs, which help them gain firsthand insights into the practices and values of various religious communities. This engagement fosters mutual respect and deepens chaplains' ability to connect with soldiers of different faiths.

Providing Inclusive Spiritual Support

One of the core responsibilities of military chaplains is to provide spiritual support that is inclusive and respectful of all beliefs. This means creating an environment where soldiers feel comfortable expressing their faith, regardless of their religious background. Chaplains achieve this by offering services and programs that accommodate the diverse spiritual needs of their units.

For example, chaplains may organize interfaith services that include prayers and readings from multiple religious traditions. They might also coordinate with lay leaders from different faiths to ensure that specific religious observances are honored. This inclusivity helps to foster a sense of unity and respect within the military community, allowing soldiers to practice their faith without fear of discrimination or exclusion.

Facilitating Religious Observances

Chaplains play a crucial role in facilitating religious observances for soldiers. This involves ensuring that soldiers have access to the necessary resources and support to practice their faith. For Christian soldiers, this might mean providing communion services, organizing Bible studies, or arranging for worship services on Sundays and religious holidays.

For Muslim soldiers, chaplains might help coordinate Jumu'ah prayers on Fridays, provide support during Ramadan fasting, and arrange for halal meals. Jewish soldiers may require assistance with observing Shabbat, celebrating Jewish holidays, and accessing kosher food. Chaplains also support soldiers who practice other faiths or spiritual traditions, ensuring that their religious needs are met.

This facilitation extends to special accommodations that allow soldiers to observe religious practices while fulfilling their military duties. Chaplains advocate for these accommodations, working with commanders and military authorities to balance operational requirements with soldiers' religious rights.

Navigating Religious Tensions and Conflicts

In a diverse military environment, religious tensions and conflicts can arise. Chaplains are often called upon to mediate and resolve these issues, promoting harmony and understanding among soldiers. This requires sensitivity, diplomacy, and a deep commitment to fairness and respect for all beliefs.

Chaplains use their skills in conflict resolution to address misunderstandings and foster dialogue between soldiers of different faiths. They may organize workshops and discussions on religious tolerance and interfaith cooperation, helping soldiers to appreciate the value of diversity and to build respectful relationships with their peers.

By promoting an atmosphere of mutual respect and understanding, chaplains help to prevent and mitigate religious conflicts, ensuring that all soldiers can serve together harmoniously.

Supporting Soldiers with No Religious Affiliation

In addition to serving soldiers of various faiths, chaplains also provide support to those who identify as atheist, agnostic, or non-religious. These soldiers may face unique challenges in a military environment that traditionally places a strong emphasis on faith and spirituality.

Chaplains offer non-religious counseling and support, addressing the moral and ethical concerns of non-religious soldiers. They create spaces where these soldiers can discuss their beliefs and values openly, without feeling marginalized or misunderstood. By respecting and supporting soldiers with no religious affiliation, chaplains demonstrate their commitment to serving all members of the military community.

Building a Culture of Respect and Inclusion

Chaplains play a vital role in building a culture of respect and inclusion within the military. They lead by example, demonstrating how to honor and celebrate religious diversity. Through their actions and words, chaplains promote the values of tolerance, empathy, and mutual respect.

Educational programs and workshops led by chaplains help to raise awareness about different religions and encourage soldiers to appreciate the richness of the military's cultural mosaic. These initiatives contribute to a more inclusive and cohesive military environment, where soldiers of all backgrounds can thrive.

Conclusion

Addressing diverse faiths and beliefs is a central challenge for military chaplains, requiring a deep understanding of different religions and a commitment to providing inclusive spiritual support. By facilitating religious observances, navigating tensions, supporting non-religious soldiers, and building a culture of respect, chaplains ensure that the spiritual needs of all soldiers are met. Their work fosters unity and mutual respect, strengthening the bonds within the military community and upholding the values of diversity and inclusion. As we continue to explore the challenges faced by military chaplains, we will see how their dedication to inclusivity and understanding makes a profound impact on the lives of those they serve.

Ethical Dilemmas and Moral Injuries

Chaplains often confront ethical dilemmas and moral injuries, both personally and in their roles as counselors and spiritual guides for soldiers. These challenges arise from the inherent conflicts between religious convictions, ethical standards, and military objectives. Chaplains must navigate these complex issues with sensitivity and wisdom, providing support and guidance to soldiers grappling with their own moral struggles.

Reconciling Religious Convictions with Military Objectives

One of the most significant ethical dilemmas chaplains face is reconciling their religious convictions with the objectives and actions of the military. The nature of military operations, which can involve violence and destruction, often conflicts with the chaplains' spiritual teachings about peace, compassion, and the sanctity of life. Chaplains must find ways to reconcile these conflicting values while maintaining their integrity and effectiveness in their roles.

To address these dilemmas, chaplains draw upon their theological training and ethical frameworks. They engage in deep reflection and prayer, seeking guidance from their faith traditions and religious texts. Additionally, chaplains often participate in discussions and seminars on ethics and morality, which help them develop nuanced understandings of complex issues.

Chaplains also serve as ethical advisors to military commanders, providing insights into the moral implications of decisions and actions. They advocate for policies and practices that align with ethical principles, striving to balance military necessity with moral considerations. This advisory role is crucial in ensuring that ethical standards are upheld within the military.

Helping Soldiers Deal with Moral Injuries

Moral injury, a term that describes the psychological distress resulting from actions that violate one's moral or ethical code, is a significant issue faced by soldiers. These injuries can occur when soldiers witness or participate in acts that conflict with their deeply held beliefs, such as harming civilians, witnessing atrocities, or making decisions that result in the loss of life. The emotional and spiritual impact of these experiences can be profound, leading to feelings of guilt, shame, and betrayal.

Chaplains play a crucial role in helping soldiers deal with moral injuries. They provide a safe and confidential space for soldiers to express their feelings and share their experiences. Through compassionate listening and empathetic support, chaplains help soldiers process their emotions and begin the journey toward healing.

Providing Spiritual and Emotional Support

Chaplains offer spiritual and emotional support tailored to the individual needs of soldiers dealing with moral injuries. This support may include prayer, scripture reading, and spiritual counseling, all aimed at helping soldiers find solace and forgiveness. Chaplains also guide soldiers in exploring their faith and reconnecting with their spiritual beliefs, which can be a source of strength and resilience.

In addition to spiritual care, chaplains provide emotional support by helping soldiers develop coping strategies and resilience. They teach techniques for managing stress, regulating emotions, and cultivating a positive outlook. These skills are essential for soldiers to rebuild their sense of self-worth and move forward from their experiences.

Facilitating Moral and Ethical Reflection

Chaplains facilitate moral and ethical reflection, helping soldiers make sense of their experiences and integrate them into their broader understanding of life and faith. This reflection process involves exploring the moral complexities of their actions, examining the context in which decisions were made, and considering the impact on their own values and beliefs.

Through guided discussions and reflective exercises, chaplains help soldiers confront their moral injuries and find meaning in their experiences. This process is critical for healing, as it allows soldiers to reconcile their actions with their ethical and spiritual frameworks, ultimately leading to personal growth and transformation.

Collaborating with Mental Health Professionals

Recognizing that moral injuries often intersect with psychological issues such as PTSD, depression, and anxiety, chaplains collaborate closely with mental health professionals. This interdisciplinary approach ensures that soldiers receive comprehensive care that addresses both the psychological and spiritual dimensions of their injuries.

Chaplains refer soldiers to mental health services when necessary and work alongside psychologists, psychiatrists, and counselors to develop integrated treatment plans. This collaboration enhances the overall effectiveness of care, providing soldiers with the support they need to heal holistically.

Advocating for Ethical Practices

Chaplains also play a proactive role in advocating for ethical practices within the military. They work to create an environment where ethical standards are upheld, and soldiers are encouraged to act with integrity and honor. This advocacy involves promoting ethical training programs, participating in policy discussions, and supporting initiatives that prioritize moral and ethical considerations.

By fostering a culture of ethics and accountability, chaplains help prevent moral injuries and ensure that soldiers are equipped to make decisions that align with their values. This proactive approach is essential in maintaining the moral fabric of the military and supporting the well-being of all service members.

Conclusion

Ethical dilemmas and moral injuries are significant challenges faced by military chaplains. Reconciling religious convictions with military objectives requires deep reflection, ethical understanding, and advocacy for moral practices. Helping soldiers deal with moral injuries involves providing spiritual and emotional support, facilitating moral reflection, and collaborating with mental health professionals. Through their dedicated efforts, chaplains play a vital role in addressing these complex issues, promoting healing and resilience, and upholding the ethical standards of the military. As we continue to explore the challenges faced by military chaplains, we will gain a deeper appreciation for their critical role in supporting the moral and spiritual well-being of soldiers.

CHAPTER 04

THE IMPACT OF CHAPLAINCY ON SOLDIERS

Case Studies and Personal Testimonials

This chapter presents real-life stories and testimonials from soldiers whose lives have been positively impacted by military chaplains. These narratives highlight the profound difference chaplains can make in the lives of those they serve, illustrating their crucial role in providing spiritual support, emotional resilience, and moral guidance.

Case Study 1: Finding Peace Amidst Chaos

Sergeant Alex Johnson, a combat veteran who served multiple tours in Afghanistan, faced immense challenges during his deployments. The constant threat of enemy fire, the loss of close comrades, and the harsh realities of combat left him emotionally scarred and struggling with PTSD. Sgt.

Johnson found it difficult to sleep, plagued by nightmares and flashbacks that haunted him daily.

One evening, while sitting alone in the camp, he encountered Chaplain Mark Thompson. Seeing Johnson's distress, Chaplain Thompson approached him with a compassionate and non-judgmental demeanor. They began talking, and Sgt. Johnson found himself opening up about his experiences and the heavy burden he carried.

Chaplain Thompson provided a listening ear and offered spiritual counseling, helping Johnson to process his emotions and find solace in his faith. They prayed together and read passages from the Bible that spoke of hope and healing. Over time, these sessions became a regular part of Sgt. Johnson's routine.

Through the chaplain's guidance and support, Sgt. Johnson began to find peace amidst the chaos. The nightmares gradually lessened, and he started to sleep better. He credits Chaplain Thompson with helping him regain his sense of purpose and stability, enabling him to continue serving with renewed strength and resilience.

Personal Testimonial: A Beacon of Hope

Private First Class Maria Lopez had always been strong in her Catholic faith, but deployment to a conflict zone tested her beliefs like never before. The isolation from her family, the daily stress of her duties, and the constant fear for her safety led her to question her faith and feel disconnected from her spiritual roots.

One Sunday, she attended a mass conducted by Chaplain Anne-Marie Sullivan. The service was held in a small, makeshift chapel, but the warmth and sincerity of Chaplain Sullivan's words touched Lopez deeply. The chaplain spoke about the power of faith to sustain and uplift, even in the most challenging times.

After the service, Lopez approached Chaplain Sullivan and shared her struggles. The chaplain offered her encouragement and practical advice on maintaining her spiritual practices despite the demanding environment. They began meeting regularly for one-on-one counseling sessions, where they prayed together and discussed ways to strengthen Lopez's faith.

Chaplain Sullivan also helped Lopez connect with other Catholic soldiers, creating a small support network within the unit. This community became a source of strength for Lopez, providing companionship and mutual encouragement.

Lopez describes Chaplain Sullivan as a beacon of hope during her darkest moments. The chaplain's support not only helped her reconnect with her faith but also provided the emotional resilience she needed to cope with the challenges of deployment. Lopez's testimonial underscores the profound impact a chaplain can have on a soldier's spiritual and emotional well-being.

Case Study 2: Moral Guidance in Times of Crisis

Captain James Nguyen faced an ethical dilemma that weighed heavily on his conscience. During a particularly intense operation, he was ordered to carry out actions that he felt conflicted with his moral and ethical values. The decision left him distressed and questioning his role as an officer.

Captain Nguyen sought the counsel of Chaplain David Kim, a respected figure known for his wisdom and ethical guidance. The chaplain listened carefully to Nguyen's concerns, providing a safe space for him to express his doubts and fears.

Chaplain Kim helped Nguyen navigate the moral complexities of his situation. They discussed the principles of just war theory and the ethical responsibilities of military officers. The chaplain offered insights from various ethical and religious perspectives, helping Nguyen to consider his actions in a broader moral context.

Through these discussions, Captain Nguyen found clarity and a renewed sense of purpose. Chaplain Kim's guidance helped him reconcile his actions with his values, providing a path forward that honored both his duties as an officer and his personal ethics. Nguyen's experience highlights the critical role of chaplains in providing moral guidance and support during times of crisis.

Personal Testimonial: Overcoming Grief and Loss

Staff Sergeant Emily Carter experienced profound grief when her close friend and fellow soldier, Sergeant Hannah Smith, was killed in action. The loss was devastating, and Carter struggled with feelings of guilt and despair. She found it difficult to carry on with her duties, haunted by memories of her friend.

Chaplain Robert Davis reached out to Carter, offering his condolences and support. He provided a compassionate presence, allowing Carter to share her pain and grief openly. Chaplain Davis conducted a memorial service for Sgt. Smith, honoring her life and providing a space for the unit to collectively mourn.

In the following weeks, Chaplain Davis continued to support Carter through regular counseling sessions. He helped her navigate the stages of grief, encouraging her to remember her friend while finding ways to honor her legacy. They discussed spiritual practices that could provide comfort, and Carter found solace in prayer and meditation.

Chaplain Davis also connected Carter with grief support resources and encouraged her to participate in group sessions with other soldiers who had experienced similar losses. These interactions helped Carter realize she was not alone in her grief and provided a supportive community to lean on.

Carter's testimonial speaks to the healing power of chaplaincy. Chaplain Davis's support helped her overcome her grief, regain her emotional balance, and find a way to move forward. His presence and guidance were instrumental in helping her heal and continue her service with renewed strength.

Conclusion

The real-life stories and testimonials presented in this chapter illustrate the profound impact military chaplains have on the lives of soldiers. Through compassionate listening, spiritual guidance, moral support, and emotional resilience, chaplains provide a lifeline to those facing the most challenging circumstances. Their presence and dedication make a significant difference, helping soldiers navigate the complexities of military life, find solace in their faith, and emerge stronger from their experiences. As we continue to explore the impact of chaplaincy, we will see how these spiritual leaders play an indispensable role in the well-being and resilience of the military community.

Mental Health and Emotional Resilience

Chaplains are instrumental in promoting mental health and emotional resilience among soldiers. Their support can help mitigate the effects of stress, trauma, and the psychological toll of combat, playing a crucial role in maintaining the overall well-being of military personnel. This chapter explores the various ways chaplains contribute to mental health and emotional resilience, highlighting their unique position within the military structure.

Providing a Safe and Confidential Space

One of the primary ways chaplains support mental health is by offering a safe and confidential space for soldiers to express their thoughts and emotions. Unlike other military personnel, chaplains are not bound by the same reporting requirements, which allows soldiers to speak freely about their struggles without fear of reprisal or career impact. This confidentiality is crucial in encouraging soldiers to seek help when they need it.

Chaplains listen with empathy and without judgment, providing soldiers with the opportunity to unburden themselves and process their experiences. This compassionate presence helps soldiers feel understood and supported, which is essential in building emotional resilience.

Crisis Intervention and Immediate Support

In times of crisis, chaplains are often among the first to respond, providing immediate emotional and spiritual support. Whether a soldier is dealing with a personal loss, a traumatic event, or overwhelming stress, chaplains are available to offer comfort and guidance. Their presence can be a stabilizing force, helping soldiers navigate acute emotional crises and preventing further deterioration of their mental health.

Chaplains are trained to recognize the signs of mental health issues, such as PTSD, depression, and anxiety. They provide initial support and, when necessary, refer soldiers to mental health professionals for further treatment. This early intervention can be critical in preventing long-term psychological damage and promoting recovery.

Stress Management and Coping Strategies

Chaplains play a vital role in teaching stress management and coping strategies. Through workshops, counseling sessions, and informal interactions, they offer practical advice on how to handle the pressures of military life. These strategies may include mindfulness techniques, relaxation exercises, and time management skills, all of which help soldiers manage stress more effectively.

Chaplains also encourage soldiers to engage in activities that promote mental and emotional well-being, such as physical exercise, hobbies, and social interactions. By fostering a balanced lifestyle, chaplains help soldiers build resilience and reduce the impact of stress on their mental health.

Spiritual Resilience and Meaning-Making

Spirituality can be a powerful source of resilience, providing soldiers with a sense of purpose and meaning, especially in the face of adversity. Chaplains help soldiers tap into their spiritual resources, offering guidance on how to strengthen their faith and find solace in their beliefs. This spiritual support can be particularly important for soldiers grappling with the moral and ethical complexities of combat.

Chaplains facilitate spiritual practices such as prayer, meditation, and religious study, which can enhance emotional resilience. They also help soldiers make sense of their experiences, finding meaning in their service and sacrifices. This process of meaning-making is crucial in helping soldiers integrate their experiences into their broader life narratives, promoting healing and growth.

Building Community and Support Networks

The sense of community and belonging is vital for mental health and emotional resilience. Chaplains play a key role in building these support networks within the military. They organize group activities, religious services, and social events that foster camaraderie and mutual support among soldiers.

By creating opportunities for soldiers to connect with one another, chaplains help build a strong sense of community. These connections provide emotional support and reduce feelings of isolation, which can be particularly important during deployments and other stressful periods.

Collaborating with Mental Health Professionals

Chaplains work closely with mental health professionals to provide comprehensive care for soldiers. This collaboration ensures that soldiers receive both spiritual and psychological support, addressing their needs holistically. Chaplains refer soldiers to mental health services when necessary and participate in multidisciplinary teams that develop and implement treatment plans.

This integrated approach enhances the effectiveness of mental health care, as it recognizes the interplay between spiritual and psychological well-being. By working together, chaplains and mental health professionals can provide more comprehensive and nuanced support, helping soldiers achieve better outcomes.

Supporting Families and Loved Ones

The well-being of soldiers is closely linked to the well-being of their families and loved ones. Chaplains extend their support to the families of military personnel, offering counseling, resources, and guidance to help them cope with the challenges of military life. This support is essential in promoting the overall resilience of soldiers, as it ensures that their families are also cared for and supported.

Chaplains provide assistance with family issues, such as relationship problems, parenting challenges, and the stresses of deployment. They offer workshops and support groups for military families, creating a community of mutual support and understanding. By supporting families, chaplains help create a stable and supportive environment for soldiers, which is crucial for their mental health and emotional resilience.

Promoting a Culture of Mental Health Awareness

Chaplains play a crucial role in promoting a culture of mental health awareness within the military. They advocate for the importance of mental health and work to reduce the stigma associated with seeking help. Through education and outreach, chaplains help soldiers understand the importance of mental health and encourage them to take proactive steps to care for their well-being.

y fostering an environment where mental health is openly discussed and prioritized, chaplains help create a military culture that supports the holistic well-being of its members. This cultural shift is essential in ensuring that soldiers feel comfortable seeking help and accessing the resources they need.

Conclusion

Chaplains are instrumental in promoting mental health and emotional resilience among soldiers. Through their compassionate presence, crisis intervention, stress management strategies, spiritual support, and community-building efforts, chaplains provide essential support that helps mitigate the effects of stress, trauma, and the psychological toll of combat. Their unique position within the military allows them to address the spiritual and emotional needs of soldiers, promoting holistic well-being and resilience. As we continue to explore the impact of chaplaincy, we will see how their dedicated efforts make a profound difference in the lives of those they serve, ensuring that soldiers have the support they need to thrive in the face of adversity.

Enhancing Morale and Cohesion

By fostering a sense of community and providing a listening ear, chaplains enhance unit morale and cohesion. Their presence can be a stabilizing force during times of uncertainty and conflict, contributing significantly to the overall effectiveness and well-being of military units. This chapter explores how chaplains play a vital role in building morale and fostering a strong sense of cohesion among soldiers.

Fostering a Sense of Community

One of the primary ways chaplains enhance morale and cohesion is by fostering a sense of community within military units. They create spaces where soldiers can come together, share their experiences, and support one another. This sense of community is crucial in a military environment, where soldiers often face isolation from their families and the civilian world.

Chaplains organize various group activities, such as religious services, prayer groups, and social events, which help build camaraderie and mutual support among soldiers. These activities provide opportunities for soldiers to connect on a deeper level, forming bonds that strengthen the unit as a whole. By promoting a sense of belonging, chaplains help create an environment where soldiers feel valued and supported.

Providing a Listening Ear

Chaplains are known for their compassionate presence and willingness to listen. They offer a non-judgmental, confidential space where soldiers can express their concerns, fears, and frustrations. This ability to listen deeply and empathetically is crucial in helping soldiers feel heard and understood.

When soldiers know that they have someone they can talk to, it alleviates feelings of loneliness and isolation. Chaplains provide a safe outlet for soldiers to vent their emotions, discuss personal problems, and seek advice. This supportive listening helps soldiers manage stress and maintain their mental and emotional well-being, which in turn enhances unit morale.

Supporting Commanders and Leaders

Chaplains also play a key role in supporting military commanders and leaders. They serve as advisors on issues related to morale, ethics, and the well-being of the troops. By providing insights into the emotional and spiritual state of the unit, chaplains help commanders make informed decisions that positively impact morale and cohesion.

Chaplains often participate in leadership meetings and planning sessions, offering a unique perspective on the needs and concerns of soldiers. Their input can help shape policies and practices that promote a healthy and supportive environment. By working closely with leaders, chaplains contribute to a command climate that prioritizes the well-being of all members.

Facilitating Communication and Understanding

Effective communication is essential for maintaining morale and cohesion within a military unit. Chaplains often act as mediators and facilitators, helping to resolve conflicts and foster understanding among soldiers. They encourage open dialogue and help soldiers navigate interpersonal issues that could otherwise undermine unit cohesion.

By promoting effective communication, chaplains help prevent misunderstandings and build trust among soldiers. This trust is a foundational element of a cohesive unit, enabling soldiers to work together more effectively and support one another in challenging situations.

Promoting Ethical and Moral Standards

Chaplains are instrumental in promoting ethical and moral standards within the military. They provide guidance on issues related to integrity, honor, and ethical behavior, helping soldiers align their actions with their values. This focus on ethics and morality fosters a culture of trust and respect within the unit.

When soldiers feel confident that their peers and leaders are committed to ethical behavior, it enhances their sense of security and trust. Chaplains reinforce these standards through training, counseling, and examples, helping to create an environment where ethical conduct is the norm.

Organizing Team-Building Activities

Chaplains organize team-building activities that strengthen bonds among soldiers and improve unit cohesion. These activities can range from spiritual retreats and workshops to recreational outings and community service projects. By participating in these events, soldiers develop a deeper sense of camaraderie and mutual support.

Team-building activities also provide opportunities for soldiers to relax and recharge, which is essential for maintaining high morale. Chaplains ensure that these activities are inclusive and cater to the diverse interests and needs of the unit, promoting a sense of unity and belonging.

Offering Crisis Support

During times of crisis, chaplains are a stabilizing force, providing crucial support that helps maintain morale and cohesion. Whether dealing with the aftermath of a traumatic event, the loss of a comrade, or other significant challenges, chaplains offer immediate and compassionate care.

Their presence during crises helps soldiers feel supported and less alone. Chaplains provide counseling, facilitate group discussions, and organize memorial services, helping the unit process their emotions and begin healing together. This support is vital in maintaining the unit's cohesion and morale during difficult times.

Conclusion

Chaplains play an indispensable role in enhancing unit morale and cohesion by fostering a sense of community, providing a listening ear, supporting leaders, facilitating communication, promoting ethical standards, organizing team-building activities, and offering crisis support. Their presence is a stabilizing force during times of uncertainty and conflict, helping soldiers feel valued, understood, and supported. As we continue to explore the impact of chaplaincy, we will see how these efforts contribute to the overall effectiveness and well-being of military units, ensuring that soldiers have the resilience and unity needed to face the challenges of their service.

CHAPTER 05

CHAPLAINCY IN DIFFERENT MILITARY CONTEXTS

Differences in Army, Navy, Air Force, and Marine Corps Chaplaincies

While the core mission of military chaplaincy—to provide spiritual support and moral guidance to service members—remains consistent, each branch of the military has unique traditions, operational environments, and requirements that shape the chaplain's role. This chapter explores the distinctive aspects of chaplaincy within the Army, Navy, Air Force, and Marine Corps, highlighting how these differences influence the duties and responsibilities of chaplains.

Army Chaplaincy

The Army, being the largest branch of the U.S. military, has a vast and diverse chaplaincy program. Army chaplains are embedded within units at all levels, from small battalions to large divisions, ensuring that spiritual support is always accessible to soldiers, regardless of their location.

Deployment and Field Ministry

Army chaplains often deploy with their units to combat zones and remote locations. This close integration means that chaplains share the same living and working conditions as the soldiers they serve, from the trenches of frontline combat to the isolation of forward operating bases. Their presence in the field allows them to provide immediate support and build strong, trusting relationships with soldiers.

Unit Cohesion and Morale

Army chaplains play a crucial role in fostering unit cohesion and morale. They organize religious services, prayer meetings, and spiritual retreats that bring soldiers together, creating a sense of community and mutual support. By participating in daily unit activities, chaplains gain a deep understanding of the soldiers' experiences and challenges, enabling them to offer relevant and timely guidance.

Navy Chaplaincy

Navy chaplains serve a diverse and dispersed community, including sailors on ships, submarines, and bases around the world. The unique maritime environment of the Navy presents distinct challenges and opportunities for chaplains.

Life at Sea

Navy chaplains often spend extended periods at sea, where they provide spiritual support to sailors in confined and isolated conditions. The close quarters and prolonged deployments can strain sailors' mental and emotional well-being, making the chaplain's role especially critical. Chaplains conduct worship services, offer counseling, and facilitate recreational activities that help maintain morale and cohesion on board.

Interfaith and Inclusivity

Given the diverse religious backgrounds of sailors, Navy chaplains must be adept at providing inclusive spiritual support. They often lead interfaith services and work with lay leaders to ensure that the religious needs of all sailors are met. This inclusive approach fosters an environment of respect and understanding, essential for maintaining harmony within the close-knit shipboard community.

Support for Marines and Coast Guardsmen

Navy chaplains also serve Marine Corps and Coast Guard personnel, reflecting the Navy's operational partnerships with these branches. This requires chaplains to be familiar with the unique cultures and challenges of each service, providing tailored support that meets their specific needs.

Air Force Chaplaincy

Air Force chaplains serve in a branch known for its technological advancements and strategic missions. The Air Force's focus on air and space superiority shapes the chaplain's role in several distinct ways.

Base Assignments and Mobility

Air Force chaplains are primarily stationed at air bases, both domestic and international. These assignments often involve working with highly specialized personnel engaged in complex and high-stress operations. Chaplains provide spiritual care, counseling, and ethical guidance, addressing the unique challenges faced by airmen and their families.

Technological Integration

The Air Force's emphasis on technology extends to its chaplaincy program. Chaplains use digital tools and platforms to reach airmen deployed in remote locations, offering virtual counseling, prayer sessions, and religious services. This innovative approach ensures that spiritual support is accessible, regardless of physical distance.

Resilience and Mental Health

Air Force chaplains play a significant role in promoting resilience and mental health. They collaborate with mental health professionals to provide comprehensive care, addressing both the spiritual and psychological needs of airmen. Chaplains lead workshops on stress management, mindfulness, and spiritual resilience, helping airmen maintain their well-being in high-pressure environments.

Marine Corps Chaplaincy

Marine Corps chaplains serve in a branch known for its rigorous physical and mental demands, as well as its strong sense of tradition and camaraderie. The Marine Corps' ethos of "Semper Fidelis" (Always Faithful) is reflected in the dedication and resilience of its chaplains.

Embedded Ministry

Marine Corps chaplains are deeply embedded within their units, often deploying alongside Marines to combat zones and austere environments. This close integration allows chaplains to experience the same challenges and dangers as the Marines they serve, fostering strong bonds of trust and respect.

Character Development and Ethical Leadership

Marine Corps chaplains play a vital role in character development and ethical leadership. They provide training on the core values of honor, courage, and commitment, helping Marines align their actions with these principles. Chaplains also offer moral guidance, assisting Marines in navigating the ethical complexities of combat and military operations.

Support for Families

Recognizing the importance of family support, Marine Corps chaplains extend their care to the families of Marines. They offer counseling, resources, and community-building activities that help families cope with the unique challenges of Marine Corps life. By supporting families, chaplains contribute to the overall resilience and stability of the Marine Corps community.

Conclusion

While the core mission of military chaplaincy is consistent across all branches of the military, the unique traditions, operational environments, and requirements of the Army, Navy, Air Force, and Marine Corps shape the chaplain's role in distinct ways. Army chaplains focus on unit cohesion and field ministry, Navy chaplains navigate life at sea and provide interfaith support, Air Force chaplains integrate technology and promote resilience, and Marine Corps chaplains emphasize character development and family support. Despite these differences, all military chaplains share a common commitment to providing spiritual care, moral guidance, and emotional support to service members, ensuring that they have the resources and resilience needed to fulfill their duties. As we continue to explore the role of chaplains, we will see how their unique contributions enhance the well-being and effectiveness of the military as a whole.

International Perspectives and Practices

Military chaplaincy is a global phenomenon, with different countries adopting various approaches to provide spiritual care and moral guidance to their service members. This section examines international practices in military chaplaincy and the lessons that can be learned from them. By exploring the diverse ways chaplaincy is implemented around the world, we can gain valuable insights into effective strategies and approaches that enhance the support provided to military personnel.

United Kingdom

The United Kingdom has a well-established tradition of military chaplaincy, with the Royal Army Chaplains' Department (RAChD) serving as one of the oldest in the world. British military chaplains, known as "Padres," are integrated into the Army, Royal Navy, and Royal Air Force.

Integrated Ministry

British military chaplains are embedded within their units, similar to their U.S. counterparts. They accompany troops on deployments and exercises, providing spiritual support and pastoral care. This close integration allows chaplains to build strong relationships with service members, fostering trust and providing timely support.

Interfaith Approach

The UK chaplaincy emphasizes an interfaith approach, recognizing the diverse religious backgrounds of service members. Chaplains from various faith traditions work together to provide inclusive spiritual care, ensuring that all personnel have access to religious support. This collaborative model promotes mutual respect and understanding among different faith groups.

Canada

The Canadian Armed Forces (CAF) have a unified chaplaincy service that serves all branches of the military. Canadian chaplains are known for their holistic approach to spiritual care, addressing the physical, emotional, and spiritual needs of service members.

Holistic Care

Canadian military chaplains emphasize holistic care, recognizing that the well-being of service members encompasses more than just their spiritual needs. Chaplains collaborate with medical and mental health professionals to provide comprehensive support, addressing the full spectrum of service members' well-being.

Multiculturalism and Inclusivity

Canada's multicultural society is reflected in its military chaplaincy. Canadian chaplains are trained to provide inclusive support that respects the diverse cultural and religious backgrounds of service members. This commitment to inclusivity ensures that all personnel feel valued and supported, regardless of their beliefs.

Australia

The Australian Defence Force (ADF) chaplaincy is known for its adaptability and focus on building resilience among service members. Australian chaplains serve in the Army, Navy, and Air Force, providing spiritual and pastoral care in various contexts.

Resilience Building

Australian military chaplains play a key role in building resilience among service members. They offer training and workshops on stress management, emotional regulation, and spiritual resilience, helping personnel develop the skills needed to cope with the challenges of military life.

Adaptive Ministry

Australian chaplains are known for their adaptability, providing spiritual support in diverse and often challenging environments. Whether on deployments, humanitarian missions, or domestic operations, chaplains adjust their approach to meet the unique needs of service members in different contexts.

Germany

The German Bundeswehr's military chaplaincy operates within a unique framework, emphasizing both spiritual care and ethical guidance. German military chaplains, known as "Militärseelsorger," serve in the Army, Navy, and Air Force.

Ethical Leadership

German military chaplains place a strong emphasis on ethical leadership. They provide training and guidance on ethical decision-making, helping service members navigate moral dilemmas and uphold the highest standards of conduct. This focus on ethics reinforces the integrity and professionalism of the Bundeswehr.

Collaborative Model

The German chaplaincy operates within a collaborative model, with chaplains from both the Protestant and Catholic traditions working together to provide comprehensive support. This ecumenical approach ensures that service members receive spiritual care that respects their diverse religious backgrounds.

Israel

The Israel Defense Forces (IDF) have a unique chaplaincy service that reflects the country's diverse religious landscape. The IDF's military rabbinate provides spiritual support and religious services to Jewish soldiers, while also respecting the needs of non-Jewish personnel.

Religious Observance and Support

The IDF's chaplaincy is deeply integrated into the religious life of soldiers, providing support for religious observance and ensuring that soldiers can practice their faith even in challenging conditions. Chaplains facilitate access to kosher food, organize prayer services, and support soldiers during religious holidays.

Inclusive Practices

While the IDF's chaplaincy primarily serves Jewish soldiers, it also provides support for non-Jewish personnel. Chaplains work to accommodate the religious needs of Christian, Muslim, and Druze soldiers, fostering an inclusive environment that respects the diverse beliefs of all service members.

South Korea

The Republic of Korea Armed Forces (ROKAF) chaplaincy reflects the country's religious diversity, with chaplains serving in the Army, Navy, and Air Force. South Korean chaplains provide spiritual care and support in a variety of settings, from combat zones to training camps.

Spiritual Resilience

South Korean military chaplains focus on enhancing the spiritual resilience of service members. They offer counseling, religious services, and spiritual training that help soldiers maintain their faith and moral strength in the face of adversity.

Cultural Sensitivity

The ROKAF chaplaincy emphasizes cultural sensitivity, recognizing the importance of respecting the diverse cultural and religious backgrounds of service members. Chaplains receive training in cultural competence, enabling them to provide effective support that honors the traditions and beliefs of all personnel.

Lessons Learned from International Practices

By examining the diverse approaches to military chaplaincy around the world, several key lessons emerge that can enhance the effectiveness of chaplaincy services:

1. Inclusivity and Interfaith Collaboration: Promoting inclusivity and fostering interfaith collaboration ensures that all service members receive respectful and comprehensive spiritual care. Chaplains can benefit from working together across religious boundaries, creating a more cohesive and supportive environment.

2. Holistic Care: Addressing the physical, emotional, and spiritual needs of service members through a holistic approach enhances overall well-being. Collaboration with medical and mental health professionals ensures that service members receive comprehensive support.

3. Resilience Building: Providing training and resources that build resilience helps service members cope with the challenges of military life. Chaplains can play a key role in promoting emotional regulation, stress management, and spiritual resilience.

4. Ethical Leadership: Emphasizing ethical leadership and decision-making reinforces the integrity and professionalism of military personnel. Chaplains can offer guidance and training that help service members navigate moral dilemmas and uphold ethical standards.

5. Adaptability: Adapting chaplaincy practices to meet the unique needs of service members in diverse contexts ensures that spiritual support is relevant and effective.

Chaplains should be prepared to adjust their approach based on the specific challenges and environments they encounter.

Conclusion

Military chaplaincy is a global phenomenon that reflects the diverse cultural and religious landscapes of different countries. By examining international practices, we can gain valuable insights into effective strategies for providing spiritual care and moral guidance to service members. The lessons learned from these diverse approaches highlight the importance of inclusivity, holistic care, resilience building, ethical leadership, and adaptability. As we continue to explore the role of chaplains, we will see how these practices can be integrated to enhance the support provided to military personnel worldwide.

The Role of Chaplains in Peacekeeping Missions

In peacekeeping missions, chaplains often play a critical role in fostering peace and reconciliation. Their efforts in these contexts highlight the importance of spiritual leadership in achieving lasting peace. This chapter explores how chaplains contribute to peacekeeping operations, the unique challenges they face, and the impact of their work on both military personnel and local communities.

Fostering Peace and Reconciliation

Chaplains in peacekeeping missions are tasked with fostering peace and reconciliation among conflicting parties. Their spiritual and ethical guidance helps build trust and understanding between opposing groups. Chaplains facilitate dialogue and mediation, encouraging conflicting parties to seek common ground and resolve their differences peacefully.

Promoting Ethical Conduct

One of the chaplain's key roles in peacekeeping missions is promoting ethical conduct among military personnel. Chaplains provide guidance on the principles of just conduct, human rights, and the treatment of civilians. By reinforcing the importance of ethical behavior, chaplains help ensure that peacekeeping forces act with integrity and respect for all individuals.

Chaplains also offer moral support to peacekeepers, helping them navigate the ethical complexities of their mission. This support is crucial in maintaining the morale and integrity of peacekeeping forces, which is essential for the success of their operations.

Supporting Local Communities

Chaplains often extend their support beyond the military, engaging with local communities to foster peace and reconciliation. They work with local religious and community leaders to build bridges and promote mutual understanding.

Chaplains participate in community outreach programs, provide humanitarian aid, and support initiatives that address the root causes of conflict.

By building relationships with local communities, chaplains help create an environment conducive to peace and stability. Their efforts contribute to the overall success of peacekeeping missions, as lasting peace can only be achieved through the active involvement and support of local populations.

Providing Spiritual and Emotional Support

Peacekeeping missions can be emotionally and spiritually challenging for military personnel. Chaplains provide essential spiritual and emotional support, helping peacekeepers cope with the stress and uncertainties of their mission. They offer counseling, conduct religious services, and provide opportunities for reflection and prayer.

This support is vital in maintaining the mental and emotional well-being of peacekeepers. Chaplains help them process their experiences, manage stress, and stay focused on their mission. By fostering resilience and morale, chaplains contribute to the overall effectiveness of peacekeeping forces.

Facilitating Interfaith Dialogue

In many peacekeeping missions, chaplains facilitate interfaith dialogue to promote understanding and cooperation among diverse religious groups. They organize interfaith services, workshops, and discussions that bring together individuals from different faith traditions. These initiatives help break down barriers, reduce mistrust, and foster a sense of shared humanity.

Chaplains' efforts in promoting interfaith dialogue are crucial in environments where religious tensions contribute to conflict. By encouraging mutual respect and understanding, chaplains help create a foundation for lasting peace and reconciliation.

Addressing Moral Injuries

Peacekeepers often face moral and ethical dilemmas that can lead to moral injuries—psychological distress resulting from actions that violate one's moral or ethical code. Chaplains play a critical role in addressing these moral injuries, providing a safe space for peacekeepers to discuss their experiences and seek guidance.

Through counseling and spiritual support, chaplains help peacekeepers process their moral injuries and find a path to healing. This support is essential in ensuring that peacekeepers can continue to serve with integrity and maintain their mental and emotional well-being.

Building a Culture of Peace

Chaplains contribute to building a culture of peace within peacekeeping forces. They emphasize the importance of non-violence, compassion, and respect for all individuals. Chaplains provide training on conflict resolution, ethical leadership, and the principles of peacebuilding.

By fostering a culture of peace, chaplains help ensure that peacekeeping forces act as positive role models and agents of change. Their leadership inspires peacekeepers to uphold the highest standards of conduct and to work towards the goal of lasting peace and reconciliation.

Conclusion

In peacekeeping missions, chaplains play a critical role in fostering peace and reconciliation. Their efforts in promoting ethical conduct, supporting local communities, providing spiritual and emotional support, facilitating interfaith dialogue, addressing moral injuries, and building a culture of peace highlight the importance of spiritual leadership in achieving lasting peace. As we continue to explore the role of chaplains, we will see how their unique contributions enhance the effectiveness of peacekeeping operations and contribute to the overall goal of creating a more peaceful and just world.

CHAPTER 06

THEOLOGICAL AND PHILOSOPHICAL UNDERPINNINGS

Faith and Duty: The Theological Basis of Chaplaincy

The work of military chaplains is deeply grounded in theological principles that emphasize service, sacrifice, and the care of souls. These principles provide the foundation for their unique role within the military, guiding their actions and shaping their mission. This chapter delves into the religious doctrines and philosophical underpinnings that inform and inspire chaplaincy, highlighting how these beliefs translate into the practical and spiritual support chaplains provide to service members.

Service and Sacrifice

At the heart of chaplaincy is the commitment to service and sacrifice, concepts that are central to many religious traditions. For Christian chaplains, this commitment is rooted in the example of Jesus Christ, who is often described as the "Good Shepherd" who lays down his life for his sheep (John 10:11). The notion of selfless service is also echoed in other religious traditions, such as the Buddhist emphasis on compassion and the Islamic principle of serving others as an act of worship.

Chaplains embody these principles through their dedication to supporting military personnel, often at great personal cost. Their willingness to share the hardships of military life, including deployment to conflict zones and separation from their families, reflects the sacrificial nature of their vocation. This selflessness is a powerful testament to their faith and commitment to the well-being of those they serve.

The Care of Souls

The primary mission of chaplains is the care of souls, a concept that encompasses the spiritual, emotional, and moral well-being of individuals. This mission is deeply rooted in religious traditions that emphasize the importance of nurturing and guiding the human spirit.

In Christianity, the care of souls is a central aspect of pastoral ministry. The Apostle Paul, in his letters, often speaks of the responsibilities of spiritual leaders to care for their congregations, providing guidance, comfort, and encouragement (1 Peter 5:2-3). Similarly, in Judaism, the role of the rabbi includes providing spiritual leadership and pastoral care, addressing both the spiritual and practical needs of the community.

For chaplains, the care of souls involves offering spiritual guidance, conducting religious services, and providing pastoral counseling. They help service members navigate the moral and ethical complexities of military life, offering support that is grounded in their religious beliefs and traditions. This holistic approach ensures that service members receive comprehensive care that addresses all aspects of their well-being.

Moral and Ethical Guidance

Chaplains play a crucial role in providing moral and ethical guidance, helping service members make decisions that align with their values and the ethical standards of their profession. This aspect of chaplaincy is informed by religious doctrines that emphasize the importance of moral integrity and ethical behavior.

In many religious traditions, ethical principles are derived from sacred texts and teachings. For example, the Ten Commandments in Judaism and Christianity, the Five Precepts in Buddhism, and the ethical teachings of the Quran in Islam provide frameworks for moral conduct. Chaplains draw on these principles to offer guidance on issues such as the just conduct of war, the treatment of non-combatants, and the responsibilities of leadership.

By reinforcing ethical standards and promoting moral reflection, chaplains help create a military culture that values integrity and accountability. Their presence serves as a constant reminder of the importance of ethical conduct, even in the most challenging circumstances.

Spiritual Resilience

Theological principles also underpin the chaplain's role in fostering spiritual resilience. Many religious traditions teach that faith can provide strength and comfort in times of adversity. This belief is encapsulated in verses such as Psalm 23:4, "Even though I walk through the valley of the shadow of death, I will fear no evil, for you are with me," and in the Quranic teaching that "Indeed, with hardship [will be] ease" (Quran 94:6).

Chaplains help service members draw on their faith to build resilience, providing spiritual practices and teachings that offer solace and strength. This support is essential in helping individuals cope with the stresses and traumas of military life, fostering a sense of hope and purpose that sustains them through difficult times.

Interfaith Respect and Collaboration

In a pluralistic military environment, chaplains must navigate and respect a wide array of religious beliefs. This commitment to interfaith respect and collaboration is grounded in theological principles that emphasize the dignity and worth of all individuals.

Many religious traditions teach the importance of loving one's neighbor and showing respect for all people, regardless of their beliefs. For example, Christianity teaches the principle of loving others as oneself (Mark 12:31), while Islam emphasizes the importance of respecting others and their faiths (Quran 49:13). This theological foundation enables chaplains to provide inclusive support that honors the diverse backgrounds of service members.

Chaplains facilitate interfaith dialogue and cooperation, creating an environment of mutual respect and understanding. This inclusive approach ensures that all service members receive the spiritual support they need, fostering unity and cohesion within the military community.

The Role of Chaplains in Ethical Decision-Making

Chaplains also play a pivotal role in ethical decision-making within the military. Their theological training equips them to address complex moral dilemmas, offering insights that help service members navigate difficult choices.

Many religious traditions include teachings on justice, mercy, and the sanctity of life, which provide valuable perspectives on ethical issues. Chaplains draw on these teachings to offer guidance on topics such as the rules of engagement, the treatment of prisoners, and the use of force. Their input helps ensure that military operations are conducted in a manner that upholds ethical standards and respects human dignity.

Conclusion

The work of military chaplains is deeply grounded in theological principles that emphasize service, sacrifice, and the care of souls. These principles provide the foundation for their unique role within the military, guiding their actions and shaping their mission. By offering spiritual guidance, moral and ethical support, and fostering resilience, chaplains play a crucial role in the well-being of service members. Their commitment to interfaith respect and collaboration further enhances their ability to provide inclusive and comprehensive support. As we continue to explore the role of chaplains, we will see how these theological underpinnings inform and inspire their work, ensuring that they remain a vital presence within the military community.

Philosophical Perspectives on War and Peace

Chaplains must grapple with complex philosophical questions about the nature of war and peace. These questions shape their understanding of their role and responsibilities within the military. This section explores various philosophical perspectives that influence chaplains' approaches to their work, providing a deeper understanding of how they navigate the ethical and moral complexities of military service.

Just War Theory

One of the most influential philosophical frameworks for understanding the ethics of war is the Just War Theory. Originating in Christian theology and developed by thinkers such as Augustine and Thomas Aquinas, the Just War Theory outlines conditions under which war can be morally justified. These conditions include just cause, legitimate authority, right intention, proportionality, and last resort.

Just Cause and Right Intention

According to Just War Theory, a war is only just if it is waged for a just cause, such as self-defense or the protection of innocent lives. Additionally, the intention behind the war must be righteous, aiming to promote peace and justice rather than seeking power or revenge. Chaplains use these principles to help soldiers and commanders evaluate the moral justification of their actions and decisions in warfare.

Proportionality and Last Resort

Just War Theory also emphasizes the principles of proportionality and last resort. Proportionality requires that the violence used in war must be proportionate to the injury suffered, and the harm caused by military action should not exceed the benefits gained. Last resort means that all non-violent alternatives must be exhausted before resorting to war. Chaplains guide service members in considering these principles when making strategic decisions, ensuring that ethical standards are upheld.

Pacifism

Pacifism is another philosophical perspective that influences some chaplains. Pacifism rejects all forms of violence and warfare, advocating for peaceful resolution of conflicts. This perspective is rooted in various religious and philosophical traditions, including Christianity, Buddhism, and Quakerism.

Moral and Ethical Dilemmas

Chaplains who align with pacifist principles face unique challenges in the military context. They must reconcile their commitment to non-violence with their duties in an institution that engages in armed conflict. These chaplains often focus on promoting peace, supporting conscientious objectors, and providing moral guidance on non-violent resistance and conflict resolution.

Promoting Peace

Even within a military framework, pacifist chaplains work to foster a culture of peace and non-violence. They advocate for diplomatic solutions, support humanitarian missions, and encourage service members to consider the broader implications of their actions. This perspective emphasizes the importance of addressing the root causes of conflict and working towards sustainable peace.

Realism

Realism is a philosophical perspective that views war as an inevitable aspect of international relations, driven by the self-interest and power dynamics of states. Realists argue that ethical considerations are secondary to the practical necessities of national security and survival.

Pragmatic Approach

Chaplains influenced by realism may adopt a more pragmatic approach to their role, focusing on the immediate needs and well-being of service members. They acknowledge the harsh realities of war and strive to provide support that helps soldiers cope with the moral and psychological challenges they face.

Balancing Ethics and Necessity

While realism emphasizes the necessity of war, chaplains still strive to balance ethical considerations with practical realities. They guide service members in making morally informed decisions, even within the constraints of military strategy and national security interests. This perspective highlights the importance of ethical reflection and moral responsibility, even in the context of pragmatic decision-making.

Utilitarianism

Utilitarianism is a consequentialist ethical theory that evaluates actions based on their outcomes, aiming to maximize overall happiness and minimize suffering. In the context of war, utilitarianism assesses the morality of military actions by considering their impact on the greatest number of people.

Cost-Benefit Analysis

Chaplains influenced by utilitarian principles may engage in cost-benefit analysis to evaluate the ethical implications of military decisions. They consider the potential consequences of actions, striving to ensure that the benefits of military interventions outweigh the harm caused. This approach requires careful reflection on the broader impact of war, including its effects on civilians, soldiers, and future generations.

Minimizing Harm

Utilitarian chaplains focus on minimizing harm and suffering in warfare. They advocate for strategies that reduce civilian casualties, promote humanitarian aid, and prioritize non-combatant protection. This perspective underscores the importance of ethical decision-making that considers the well-being of all affected parties.

Virtue Ethics

Virtue ethics, rooted in the philosophy of Aristotle, emphasizes the development of moral character and the pursuit of virtuous living. This perspective focuses on the cultivation of virtues such as courage, justice, compassion, and wisdom, guiding individuals to act in accordance with their moral character.

Moral Character and Leadership

Chaplains influenced by virtue ethics emphasize the importance of moral character and ethical leadership. They encourage service members to cultivate virtues that guide their actions and decisions, both in and out of combat. This approach promotes personal integrity and ethical conduct, fostering a culture of moral excellence within the military.

Role Modeling and Mentorship

Virtue ethics highlights the role of chaplains as moral role models and mentors. Chaplains lead by example, demonstrating virtuous behavior and providing guidance on ethical living. They support service members in their moral development, helping them navigate the complexities of military service with integrity and honor.

Conclusion

Chaplains must grapple with complex philosophical questions about the nature of war and peace, drawing on various ethical frameworks to guide their actions and support service members. Just War Theory provides principles for evaluating the morality of warfare, while pacifism emphasizes non-violence and peacebuilding. Realism offers a pragmatic approach, and utilitarianism focuses on maximizing overall well-being. Virtue ethics underscores the importance of moral character and ethical leadership. By integrating these philosophical perspectives, chaplains navigate the ethical and moral complexities of their role, providing valuable guidance and support to service members. As we continue to explore the role of chaplains, we will see how these philosophical underpinnings inform their work, ensuring that they remain a vital presence within the military community.

Balancing Secular and Religious Responsibilities

Military chaplains often navigate the delicate balance between their religious duties and the secular demands of military life. This balance is crucial in ensuring that chaplains can serve all soldiers effectively, regardless of their personal beliefs. This chapter explores the challenges and strategies chaplains employ to maintain this equilibrium, highlighting how they integrate their spiritual mission with their responsibilities within the military structure.

Understanding the Dual Role

Chaplains are both religious leaders and commissioned officers, a dual role that requires them to serve the spiritual needs of soldiers while also fulfilling their duties within the military hierarchy. This dual responsibility means that chaplains must adhere to military regulations and protocols while providing religious services, counseling, and spiritual guidance.

Navigating Secular Demands

The military operates within a framework of secular policies and procedures that are designed to maintain order, discipline, and effectiveness. Chaplains must respect and operate within this framework, ensuring that their religious activities do not interfere with military operations or the rights of service members who do not share their beliefs.

Chaplains participate in regular military duties, such as attending briefings, participating in training exercises, and supporting the chain of command. By engaging in these secular activities, chaplains demonstrate their commitment to the military mission and build credibility and trust among their peers and superiors.

Providing Inclusive Spiritual Care

A key aspect of balancing secular and religious responsibilities is providing inclusive spiritual care that respects the diverse beliefs of all service members. Chaplains must be sensitive to the fact that they serve soldiers from a wide range of religious backgrounds, as well as those who may be atheists or agnostics.

Chaplains offer a variety of services and support that cater to different spiritual needs, including interfaith worship services, prayer groups, and discussion forums. They also provide counseling and support that is not explicitly religious, focusing on the emotional and psychological well-being of service members.

Adhering to Ethical Standards

Chaplains must adhere to both religious and military ethical standards, which can sometimes be in tension. For example, the confidentiality of pastoral counseling is a fundamental principle in many religious traditions, but military regulations may require the reporting of certain information. Chaplains navigate these ethical dilemmas by carefully considering the implications of their actions and seeking guidance from both religious and military authorities.

Advocating for Religious Accommodation

One of the chaplain's roles is to advocate for the religious rights and accommodations of service members. This can involve requesting time and space for religious observances, ensuring access to religious materials, and facilitating dietary accommodations for religious reasons. Chaplains work with commanders and military authorities to balance these requests with the operational requirements of the military.

By advocating for religious accommodation, chaplains help create an environment where all service members can practice their faith freely and without discrimination. This advocacy is a critical component of maintaining the balance between secular and religious responsibilities.

Building Relationships and Trust

Effective chaplaincy depends on building strong relationships and trust within the military community. Chaplains must demonstrate that they are committed to the well-being of all service members, regardless of their beliefs. This requires chaplains to be approachable, empathetic, and respectful of diverse perspectives.

Chaplains build trust by being present and engaged in the daily lives of service members, participating in both religious and secular activities. By showing that they are invested in the overall mission and well-being of the unit, chaplains foster a sense of mutual respect and trust.

Training and Professional Development

To effectively balance their secular and religious responsibilities, chaplains undergo rigorous training and professional development. This includes theological education, military training, and ongoing professional development courses. Chaplains are trained to understand the complexities of military life and to provide support that is both spiritually grounded and contextually relevant.

Professional development also includes training in interfaith dialogue, cultural competence, and ethical decision-making. These skills enable chaplains to navigate the diverse and dynamic environment of the military, ensuring that they can serve all service members effectively.

Engaging with the Broader Community

Chaplains often serve as liaisons between the military and the broader civilian religious community. They engage with local religious leaders, participate in community events, and facilitate programs that connect service members with civilian religious resources. This engagement helps bridge the gap between the military and civilian worlds, providing additional support and resources for service members and their families.

Maintaining Personal Spiritual Practices

To effectively serve others, chaplains must also attend to their own spiritual well-being. This involves maintaining personal spiritual practices, seeking support from their religious communities, and engaging in self-care activities. By nurturing their own faith and well-being, chaplains ensure that they have the strength and resilience to support others.

Conclusion

Balancing secular and religious responsibilities is a fundamental aspect of military chaplaincy. Chaplains navigate this balance by understanding their dual role, providing inclusive spiritual care, adhering to ethical standards, advocating for religious accommodation, building relationships and trust, undergoing rigorous training, engaging with the broader community, and maintaining their personal spiritual practices. This delicate balance ensures that chaplains can effectively serve all soldiers, regardless of their personal beliefs, while fulfilling their duties within the military structure. As we continue to explore the role of chaplains, we will see how this balance enhances their ability to provide comprehensive and compassionate support to service members.

CHAPTER 07

TRAINING AND PREPARATION FOR MILITARY CHAPLAINCY

Pathways to Becoming a Military Chaplain

Becoming a military chaplain requires a specific educational and vocational path that combines theological education, denominational endorsement, and military training. This chapter outlines the necessary steps for individuals aspiring to serve as military chaplains, providing a comprehensive guide to the preparation and qualifications needed for this unique and demanding role.

Theological Education

The first step toward becoming a military chaplain is obtaining a solid foundation in theological education. This typically involves completing a bachelor's degree followed by a Master of Divinity (M.Div.) or an equivalent degree from an accredited seminary or divinity school. Theological education provides the academic and spiritual grounding necessary for chaplaincy, covering subjects such as biblical studies, theology, ethics, pastoral care, and religious history.

Bachelor's Degree

Aspiring chaplains usually begin with a bachelor's degree in a related field such as religious studies, theology, philosophy, or psychology. This undergraduate education lays the groundwork for advanced theological studies and helps students develop critical thinking and analytical skills.

Master of Divinity (M.Div.)

The M.Div. is the standard professional degree for chaplains, typically requiring three to four years of study. The curriculum includes coursework in theology, pastoral counseling, homiletics (preaching), liturgy, and religious education. Students also engage in practical training through internships or supervised ministry experiences, which provide hands-on opportunities to develop pastoral skills.

Denominational Endorsement

After completing theological education, prospective chaplains must obtain endorsement from their religious denomination or faith group. Denominational endorsement is a formal recognition that the individual is qualified and authorized to serve as a chaplain within that religious tradition. This endorsement process varies by denomination but generally includes the following steps:

Ordination

Many denominations require chaplains to be ordained clergy. Ordination is the process by which an individual is consecrated and authorized to perform religious rites and provide spiritual leadership. The requirements for ordination vary by denomination but typically include a combination of theological education, ministerial experience, and approval by denominational authorities.

Endorsement Application

Prospective chaplains must submit an application for endorsement to their denominational endorsing body. This application usually includes transcripts, letters of recommendation, a statement of faith, and documentation of ministerial experience. The endorsing body evaluates the application to ensure that the candidate meets the denomination's standards for chaplaincy.

Interview and Assessment

Some denominations require candidates to undergo an interview and assessment process. This may involve meetings with denominational leaders, psychological evaluations, and evaluations of the candidate's theological knowledge and pastoral skills. The goal is to assess the candidate's readiness for chaplaincy and their ability to represent the denomination effectively.

Military Training and Commissioning

Once theological education and denominational endorsement are secured, candidates must complete military training and receive a commission as a military officer. The process of joining the military as a chaplain includes several key steps:

Application and Selection

Candidates apply to the chaplaincy program of the specific branch of the military they wish to serve in—Army, Navy, Air Force, or Marine Corps. The application process includes submitting educational transcripts, endorsement documentation, and other required materials. Candidates also undergo a selection process that assesses their physical fitness, medical qualifications, and suitability for military service.

Officer Training School (OTS)

Selected candidates attend Officer Training School (OTS) or an equivalent program specific to their branch of service. OTS provides basic military training for newly commissioned officers, covering subjects such as military customs and courtesies, leadership, physical fitness, and the roles and responsibilities of military officers.

Chaplain Basic Officer Leader Course (CHBOLC)

After completing OTS, chaplain candidates attend the Chaplain Basic Officer Leader Course (CHBOLC) or its equivalent. This specialized training program focuses on the unique aspects of military chaplaincy, including military ethics, religious support operations, pastoral care in a military context, and the integration of religious support within the broader mission of the military.

Continuing Education and Professional Development

Military chaplains are expected to engage in continuing education and professional development throughout their careers. This ongoing training ensures that chaplains remain current in their theological knowledge, pastoral skills, and understanding of military operations. Continuing education opportunities may include:

Advanced Military Training

Chaplains may participate in advanced military training programs that focus on specific aspects of military operations, leadership, and chaplaincy. These programs enhance chaplains' ability to provide effective spiritual support in diverse and challenging environments.

Clinical Pastoral Education (CPE)

Many chaplains pursue Clinical Pastoral Education (CPE), a form of professional training that focuses on the development of pastoral care skills in clinical settings such as hospitals, prisons, and counseling centers. CPE programs provide supervised, hands-on experience in providing spiritual care to individuals facing crisis and trauma.

Theological Conferences and Workshops

Chaplains are encouraged to attend theological conferences, workshops, and seminars that offer opportunities for continued learning and professional growth. These events provide forums for chaplains to engage with contemporary theological issues, share best practices, and network with other religious professionals.

Conclusion

Becoming a military chaplain requires a specific educational and vocational path that includes theological education, denominational endorsement, and military training. This comprehensive preparation ensures that chaplains are well-equipped to provide spiritual care, moral guidance, and emotional support to service members in diverse and challenging contexts. By engaging in ongoing professional development, chaplains maintain their skills and knowledge, ensuring that they can continue to serve effectively throughout their careers. As we continue to explore the role of chaplains, we will see how this rigorous preparation and commitment to lifelong learning enhance their ability to provide compassionate and effective support to the military community.

Training Programs and Institutions

Various institutions and programs offer specialized training for military chaplains, providing them with the skills and knowledge necessary to effectively support service members. This section provides an overview of these programs and the essential competencies they impart to future chaplains.

Seminaries and Divinity Schools

Theological education forms the foundation of a chaplain's training, and many seminaries and divinity schools offer programs tailored to the needs of future military chaplains. These institutions provide rigorous academic and practical training, covering a broad range of theological and pastoral topics.

Key Institutions

- Princeton Theological Seminary: Known for its strong emphasis on Reformed theology, Princeton offers a Master of Divinity (M.Div.) program that includes courses in pastoral care, ethics, and theology, which are essential for military chaplaincy.

- Duke Divinity School: Duke's M.Div. program integrates rigorous academic study with practical ministry training, preparing students for diverse pastoral roles, including military chaplaincy.

- Liberty University School of Divinity: Liberty offers an M.Div. program with a concentration in military chaplaincy, providing specialized courses in military ethics, pastoral counseling, and crisis intervention.

- Catholic University of America: Known for its comprehensive theological education, the university offers programs that prepare chaplains to serve in various capacities within the military, emphasizing Catholic social teaching and pastoral care.

Clinical Pastoral Education (CPE)

Clinical Pastoral Education (CPE) is a crucial component of chaplaincy training, providing hands-on experience in delivering pastoral care in clinical settings. CPE programs are offered by hospitals, counseling centers, and theological schools and are essential for developing practical skills in pastoral counseling and crisis intervention.

Key CPE Providers

- Association for Clinical Pastoral Education (ACPE): ACPE accredits CPE programs across the United States, offering standardized training that includes supervised pastoral care, reflective practice, and peer feedback.

- Veterans Affairs (VA) Hospitals: Many VA hospitals offer CPE programs specifically designed for military chaplains, focusing on the unique needs of veterans and active-duty service members.

- Major Medical Centers: Institutions such as Johns Hopkins Hospital and Massachusetts General Hospital provide CPE programs that offer diverse clinical experiences, including trauma care, mental health, and end-of-life care.

Military Chaplain Schools and Training Centers

Each branch of the U.S. military has its own chaplain school or training center that provides specialized instruction for chaplains. These institutions offer comprehensive programs that cover the unique aspects of military chaplaincy, including military ethics, religious support operations, and leadership.

Army Chaplain Center and School (USACHCS)

Located at Fort Jackson, South Carolina, USACHCS offers the Chaplain Basic Officer Leader Course (CHBOLC) and advanced training programs. The curriculum includes military ministry, pastoral care in combat, ethical leadership, and the integration of religious support within military operations.

Naval Chaplaincy School and Center (NCSC)

Located in Newport, Rhode Island, NCSC trains chaplains for service in the Navy, Marine Corps, and Coast Guard. The training focuses on the unique maritime and expeditionary environments, including shipboard ministry, crisis response, and religious accommodation.

Air Force Chaplain Corps College

Located at Maxwell Air Force Base, Alabama, this institution provides training for Air Force chaplains. The program includes courses in spiritual resilience, religious diversity, ethical decision-making, and the role of chaplains within the Air Force structure.

Marine Corps Chaplaincy Training

Marine Corps chaplains receive their initial training at the Naval Chaplaincy School and Center, followed by additional training specific to the Marine Corps. This training emphasizes the unique demands of serving with Marine units, including deployment readiness, combat ministry, and support for Marine families.

Specialized Training Programs

In addition to foundational training, military chaplains have access to specialized programs that enhance their skills in specific areas of ministry. These programs address topics such as trauma counseling, moral injury, and interfaith dialogue.

Trauma and Resilience Training

Programs such as the Trauma and Resilience Initiative offered by the Military Chaplains Association provide chaplains with advanced skills in addressing trauma and promoting resilience among service members. This training includes techniques for trauma-informed care, stress management, and spiritual recovery.

Moral Injury Programs

Institutions like the Soul Repair Center at Brite Divinity School offer programs focused on understanding and addressing moral injury. These programs provide chaplains with tools to help service members process ethical and moral dilemmas, fostering healing and reconciliation.

Interfaith and Cultural Competence Training

Organizations such as the Interfaith Center of New York offer training programs that enhance chaplains' ability to navigate religious diversity and provide inclusive spiritual care. These programs cover interfaith dialogue, cultural competence, and the promotion of religious tolerance within military settings.

Continuing Education and Professional Development

To maintain their effectiveness and stay current with best practices, military chaplains engage in ongoing continuing education and professional development. This includes attending conferences, workshops, and seminars that offer opportunities for learning and networking.

Key Conferences and Seminars

- Military Chaplains Association (MCA) Annual Conference: This conference provides chaplains with updates on current issues, professional development sessions, and opportunities to connect with peers and experts in the field.

- National Conference on Ministry to the Armed Forces (NCMAF): NCMAF offers training and resources for chaplains from various religious traditions, focusing on best practices in military chaplaincy.

- American Association of Pastoral Counselors (AAPC): AAPC offers continuing education programs that enhance chaplains' counseling skills, focusing on pastoral care, ethics, and mental health.

Conclusion

Various institutions and programs offer specialized training for military chaplains, providing them with the skills and knowledge necessary to effectively support service members. From theological education and Clinical Pastoral Education to specialized military training and ongoing professional development, these programs equip chaplains with the competencies they need to navigate the complex and demanding environment of military service. As we continue to explore the role of chaplains, we will see how this comprehensive training prepares them to provide compassionate and effective support to the military community.

Continuous Education and Development

The role of a military chaplain is dynamic and multifaceted, necessitating ongoing education and development to remain effective and relevant in their service. Continuous learning ensures that chaplains are well-equipped to address the evolving needs of military personnel and adapt to changes in military and societal contexts. This chapter explores opportunities for continuous education and professional growth available to military chaplains.

Importance of Continuous Education

Continuous education is crucial for military chaplains to stay current with theological developments, pastoral care techniques, and the latest best practices in military chaplaincy. This ongoing learning process helps chaplains to:

- Enhance their pastoral and counseling skills.

- Deepen their theological and ethical understanding.

- Stay informed about new research and developments in mental health and trauma care.

- Maintain professional licensure and endorsements.

- Foster personal and spiritual growth.

Advanced Military Training Programs

Advanced military training programs provide chaplains with specialized knowledge and skills that go beyond initial training. These programs often focus on leadership development, advanced pastoral care techniques, and the integration of new military policies and technologies.

Army Advanced Chaplain Training

The U.S. Army offers advanced training programs for chaplains at different stages of their careers. This includes the Chaplain Captain Career Course (C4) and the Chaplain Major Course (CMC), which focus on leadership, ethics, and strategic planning.

Navy and Marine Corps Advanced Training

The Naval Chaplaincy School and Center offers advanced courses for chaplains, including the Senior Leadership Course, which prepares chaplains for higher levels of command and responsibility.

Air Force Advanced Chaplain Corps College

The Air Force provides advanced training through its Chaplain Corps College, offering courses in strategic leadership, pastoral care, and resilience training for chaplains at different career stages.

Clinical Pastoral Education (CPE) and Specialized Certification

Clinical Pastoral Education (CPE) remains a vital component of a chaplain's ongoing professional development. CPE programs offer advanced training in pastoral care, focusing on areas such as trauma, grief, and crisis intervention.

Advanced CPE Programs

Chaplains can enroll in advanced CPE programs to further develop their clinical skills. These programs are often hosted by hospitals, military medical centers, and accredited CPE institutions.

Specialized Certifications

Chaplains may also pursue specialized certifications in areas such as trauma counseling, substance abuse counseling, and marriage and family therapy. Organizations such as the National Association of Catholic Chaplains (NACC) and the Association of Professional Chaplains (APC) offer certification programs that enhance chaplains' professional credentials and expertise.

Professional Conferences and Workshops

Attending professional conferences and workshops allows chaplains to stay current with the latest developments in their field, network with peers, and gain new insights and skills.

Military Chaplains Association (MCA) Annual Conference

The MCA Annual Conference offers sessions on a wide range of topics relevant to military chaplaincy, including ethical issues, pastoral care strategies, and updates on military policies.

National Conference on Ministry to the Armed Forces (NCMAF)

NCMAF provides training and resources for chaplains from various religious traditions, focusing on best practices in military chaplaincy and interfaith dialogue.

American Association of Pastoral Counselors (AAPC) Workshops

AAPC workshops provide continuing education opportunities for chaplains, focusing on pastoral care, ethics, and mental health. These workshops offer practical skills and theoretical knowledge that enhance chaplains' ability to support service members.

Online Learning and Distance Education

Online learning and distance education provide flexible and accessible options for chaplains to continue their education while serving in various locations. Many institutions offer online courses and degree programs in theology, pastoral care, and counseling.

Liberty University Online

Liberty University offers a range of online programs tailored to the needs of chaplains, including a Master of Divinity (M.Div.) with a concentration in military chaplaincy and various certificate programs in pastoral care.

Regent University Online

Regent University provides online courses in theology, ministry, and leadership, allowing chaplains to pursue advanced degrees and certifications while maintaining their duties.

Professional Reading and Self-Study

Continuous education for chaplains also includes self-directed learning through professional reading and self-study. Chaplains are encouraged to engage with current literature in theology, ethics, pastoral care, and military studies.

Recommended Reading Lists

Many military chaplaincy programs provide recommended reading lists that include essential texts in theology, pastoral care, and military ethics. Chaplains can use these lists as a guide for their self-study efforts.

Subscription to Professional Journals

Subscribing to professional journals such as the "Journal of Pastoral Care & Counseling" and the "Military

Chaplain" helps chaplains stay informed about the latest research, trends, and discussions in their field.

Mentorship and Peer Support

Mentorship and peer support are critical components of a chaplain's ongoing professional development. Experienced chaplains provide guidance, support, and encouragement to newer chaplains, helping them navigate the challenges of military ministry.

Formal Mentorship Programs

Many military branches have formal mentorship programs that pair new chaplains with experienced mentors. These programs provide structured support and opportunities for professional growth and development.

Informal Peer Networks

Informal peer networks, such as local chaplain groups and online forums, offer chaplains opportunities to connect with colleagues, share experiences, and seek advice. These networks foster a sense of community and mutual support among chaplains.

Spiritual Retreats and Personal Renewal

Maintaining personal spiritual health is essential for chaplains to remain effective in their roles. Spiritual retreats and personal renewal activities provide opportunities for chaplains to recharge and deepen their faith.

Spiritual Retreat Centers

Many religious organizations and denominations offer spiritual retreat centers where chaplains can spend time in reflection, prayer, and study. These retreats provide a break from the demands of military life and help chaplains renew their commitment to their ministry.

Personal Spiritual Practices

Chaplains are encouraged to engage in regular personal spiritual practices, such as prayer, meditation, and scripture study. These practices help chaplains maintain their spiritual resilience and stay connected to their faith traditions.

Conclusion

Continuous education and development are essential for military chaplains to remain effective and relevant in their service. Through advanced military training, Clinical Pastoral Education, professional conferences, online learning, self-study, mentorship, and spiritual renewal, chaplains can enhance their skills, deepen their knowledge, and maintain their personal and professional growth. As we continue to explore the role of chaplains, we will see how their commitment to lifelong learning ensures they can provide compassionate and effective support to the military community.

CHAPTER 08

THE FUTURE OF MILITARY CHAPLAINCY

Emerging Trends and Technologies

As warfare and society evolve, so too does the role of the military chaplain. This chapter examines emerging trends and technologies that are shaping the future of chaplaincy, from virtual ministry to the use of social media. Understanding these developments is crucial for preparing chaplains to meet the changing needs of service members and to continue providing effective spiritual and emotional support.

Virtual Ministry and Telechaplaincy

The advent of digital communication technologies has revolutionized the way chaplains can provide support to service members. Virtual ministry, or telechaplaincy, allows chaplains to reach service members regardless of their physical location, ensuring continuous access to spiritual care.

Telecounseling and Online Support Groups

Chaplains can use video conferencing tools to offer telecounseling sessions, providing pastoral care and counseling to service members who may be deployed or stationed in remote locations. Online support groups facilitate community and peer support, enabling service members to share experiences and find solidarity even when geographically dispersed.

Virtual Worship Services

Virtual worship services allow chaplains to conduct religious ceremonies and services online, ensuring that service members can participate in communal worship regardless of their deployment status. This approach also supports interfaith and multidenominational services, making religious observance more inclusive and accessible.

Social Media and Digital Outreach

Social media platforms and other digital tools offer new avenues for chaplains to connect with service members, share resources, and provide spiritual guidance.

Engaging with Service Members

Chaplains can use social media to engage with service members, offering daily reflections, inspirational messages, and updates on religious services and events. Platforms like Facebook, Instagram, and Twitter enable chaplains to maintain an active online presence, fostering a sense of connection and community.

Digital Resources and Apps

The development of religious and spiritual apps provides chaplains with tools to offer daily prayers, scripture readings, and meditation exercises. These digital resources can be tailored to the needs of individual service members, supporting their spiritual growth and resilience.

Artificial Intelligence and Chatbots

Emerging technologies like artificial intelligence (AI) and chatbots have the potential to enhance chaplaincy by providing immediate, accessible support and resources.

AI-Powered Chatbots

AI-powered chatbots can offer basic pastoral care and spiritual guidance, answering common questions, providing scriptural references, and offering prayers. While not a replacement for human chaplains, these chatbots can supplement chaplaincy services, especially during times of high demand or when chaplains are not immediately available.

Predictive Analytics

AI and predictive analytics can help chaplains identify service members who may be at risk of mental health issues or spiritual crises. By analyzing data such as deployment histories, social interactions, and health records, these technologies can provide early warning signs, enabling chaplains to intervene proactively.

Enhanced Training Through Virtual Reality (VR)

Virtual reality (VR) offers innovative training opportunities for chaplains, allowing them to simulate various pastoral care scenarios and develop their skills in a controlled environment.

Simulated Training Environments

VR can create realistic training environments where chaplains can practice providing support during combat, counseling in crisis situations, and conducting religious services in diverse settings. These simulations help chaplains build confidence and competence, preparing them for real-world challenges.

Immersive Learning Experiences

VR can also facilitate immersive learning experiences, such as virtual visits to historical religious sites or interactive lessons on different faith traditions. These experiences enhance chaplains' cultural competence and deepen their understanding of global religious contexts.

Ethical and Moral Considerations

As chaplaincy integrates new technologies, it is essential to address the ethical and moral considerations that arise. Chaplains must ensure that these technologies are used in ways that respect privacy, maintain confidentiality, and uphold the dignity of service members.

Privacy and Confidentiality

Chaplains must navigate the ethical implications of using digital platforms and AI, ensuring that service members' personal information and interactions remain confidential and secure. This requires implementing robust data protection measures and adhering to ethical guidelines.

Human Touch in Digital Ministry

While technology can enhance chaplaincy, it is crucial to maintain the human touch that is central to pastoral care. Chaplains must balance the use of digital tools with personal interactions, ensuring that technology serves to support, not replace, the personal connections that are fundamental to their role.

Interdisciplinary Collaboration

The future of military chaplaincy will increasingly involve interdisciplinary collaboration, integrating insights and expertise from fields such as psychology, sociology, and technology.

Collaborating with Mental Health Professionals

Chaplains will continue to work closely with mental health professionals to provide holistic care that addresses both spiritual and psychological needs. This collaboration ensures comprehensive support for service members, particularly those dealing with trauma, stress, or mental health issues.

Engaging with Technologists and Data Scientists

Chaplains can benefit from collaborating with technologists and data scientists to develop and implement new tools and platforms. This interdisciplinary approach ensures that technological innovations are designed with an understanding of pastoral needs and ethical considerations.

Conclusion

As warfare and society evolve, the role of the military chaplain must also adapt to meet new challenges and opportunities. Emerging trends and technologies such as virtual ministry, social media outreach, AI, VR training, and interdisciplinary collaboration are shaping the future of chaplaincy. By embracing these innovations while maintaining a focus on ethical considerations and personal connections, chaplains can continue to provide effective and compassionate support to service members. As we look to the future, the ongoing development and integration of these trends will ensure that military chaplaincy remains a vital and dynamic presence within the military community.

Adapting to Changing Warfare and Soldier Needs

Modern warfare presents new challenges and opportunities for military chaplains. As the nature of conflict evolves and the needs of soldiers change, chaplains must adapt their approaches to continue providing essential spiritual support. This chapter explores how chaplains can respond to these changes, ensuring their ministry remains relevant and effective in the face of modern military realities.

Understanding Modern Warfare

Modern warfare is characterized by technological advancements, asymmetrical conflicts, and complex geopolitical landscapes. These elements create unique challenges for military chaplains, who must navigate the spiritual and emotional impacts of these new forms of conflict.

Technological Advancements

The integration of advanced technologies such as drones, cyber warfare, and artificial intelligence into military operations has transformed the battlefield. Chaplains must understand these technologies and their implications for soldiers' experiences, including the psychological effects of remote warfare and the ethical dilemmas posed by autonomous systems.

Asymmetrical Conflicts

Asymmetrical conflicts, where state and non-state actors engage in irregular warfare, present distinct challenges. Chaplains must address the moral and psychological complexities faced by soldiers operating in these environments, including issues related to combat stress, civilian interactions, and the ambiguity of enemy combatants.

Complex Geopolitical Landscapes

Modern conflicts often involve complex geopolitical dynamics, including cultural and religious tensions. Chaplains need to be culturally competent and sensitive to the diverse backgrounds of both soldiers and local populations, fostering understanding and promoting ethical conduct in diverse settings.

Responding to New Soldier Needs

The evolving nature of soldier demographics and needs requires chaplains to adapt their approaches to ministry. This includes addressing the unique challenges faced by diverse service members and providing support that reflects the realities of modern military life.

Supporting a Diverse Force

The military is increasingly diverse, with service members from varied cultural, religious, and socioeconomic backgrounds. Chaplains must be adept at providing inclusive spiritual care that respects and honors this diversity. This involves understanding different religious practices, offering interfaith support, and advocating for religious accommodation.

Mental Health and Resilience

The mental health needs of soldiers are more prominent than ever, with increased awareness of issues such as PTSD, depression, and anxiety. Chaplains play a critical role in promoting mental health and resilience, offering counseling, support groups, and stress management resources. They also work closely with mental health professionals to provide comprehensive care.

Family Support

The impact of modern military service extends to soldiers' families, who face challenges such as frequent relocations, extended deployments, and the stress of separation. Chaplains provide support to families through counseling, family retreats, and programs designed to strengthen family resilience and cohesion.

Adapting Chaplaincy Practices

To remain effective in the context of modern warfare, chaplains must continuously adapt their practices and approaches to ministry. This involves leveraging new technologies, developing innovative programs, and engaging in continuous professional development.

Leveraging Technology

Chaplains can use technology to enhance their ministry, offering virtual counseling sessions, online worship services, and digital resources. These tools enable chaplains to reach service members regardless of their location, ensuring continuous access to spiritual support.

Developing Innovative Programs

Chaplains can develop programs that address the specific needs of modern soldiers, such as resilience training, moral injury recovery, and ethical leadership development. These programs provide soldiers with the skills and support they need to navigate the challenges of military service.

Engaging in Professional Development

Continuous professional development is essential for chaplains to stay current with best practices and emerging trends. This includes attending conferences, participating in training programs, and pursuing advanced degrees or certifications. By engaging in lifelong learning, chaplains can enhance their skills and remain effective in their ministry.

Promoting Ethical Leadership

In the context of modern warfare, ethical leadership is more important than ever. Chaplains play a vital role in promoting ethical conduct and moral decision-making among military personnel.

Ethical Decision-Making Training

Chaplains can provide training on ethical decision-making, helping soldiers navigate the complex moral landscapes of modern conflicts. This training includes discussions on the just war theory, rules of engagement, and the ethical use of technology in warfare.

Moral Leadership Development

Chaplains can foster moral leadership by mentoring and supporting commanders and other leaders. By promoting values such as integrity, compassion, and justice, chaplains help cultivate a culture of ethical leadership within the military.

Advocating for Justice and Human Rights

Chaplains have a responsibility to advocate for justice and human rights, both within the military and in the broader context of military operations.

Supporting Humanitarian Missions

Chaplains can support humanitarian missions and initiatives that promote peace and justice. This includes advocating for the protection of civilians, supporting efforts to rebuild communities affected by conflict, and promoting reconciliation and healing.

Addressing Ethical Violations

Chaplains must be prepared to address ethical violations and support efforts to hold individuals accountable for misconduct. This involves providing counsel to those affected by ethical breaches, advocating for transparency and justice, and supporting restorative practices.

Conclusion

Modern warfare and the changing needs of soldiers present new challenges and opportunities for military chaplains. By understanding the dynamics of modern conflicts, responding to the diverse needs of service members, adapting their practices, promoting ethical leadership, and advocating for justice, chaplains can continue to provide essential spiritual support. As the role of chaplains evolves, their commitment to serving and supporting soldiers in the context of modern military realities ensures that they remain a vital and dynamic presence within the military community.

The Role of Chaplains in Cyber Warfare and Remote Operations

With the rise of cyber warfare and remote operations, military chaplains must find new ways to connect with and support soldiers. These modern forms of conflict present unique challenges that require innovative approaches to ministry. This chapter explores how chaplains are adapting their roles to meet the demands of cyber warfare and remote operations, ensuring that they continue to provide essential spiritual and emotional support.

Understanding Cyber Warfare and Remote Operations

Cyber warfare and remote operations involve the use of advanced technologies to conduct military actions from a distance. These operations include cyber attacks, surveillance, and the use of unmanned systems such as drones. The nature of these conflicts can lead to distinct psychological and ethical challenges for service members involved in these operations.

Psychological Impact of Remote Operations

Service members engaged in cyber warfare and remote operations often experience a different kind of stress compared to traditional combat. The separation from the physical battlefield can lead to feelings of isolation and detachment. Additionally, the knowledge that their actions can have significant, far-reaching consequences can create unique ethical and emotional burdens.

Ethical Challenges

Cyber warfare and remote operations raise complex ethical issues, such as the implications of autonomous systems, the potential for collateral damage, and the blurred lines between combatants and non-combatants. Chaplains play a crucial role in helping service members navigate these moral dilemmas and maintain their ethical integrity.

Innovative Approaches to Chaplaincy

To effectively support service members in the context of cyber warfare and remote operations, chaplains are adopting innovative approaches to ministry that leverage technology and new methods of engagement.

Virtual Chaplaincy

Virtual chaplaincy involves using digital platforms to provide spiritual care and counseling. Chaplains can connect with service members through video conferencing, social media, and secure messaging applications, ensuring continuous support regardless of geographical location.

Telecounseling

Telecounseling allows chaplains to offer one-on-one counseling sessions through video calls. This approach is particularly effective for service members involved in remote operations, who may not have access to on-site chaplaincy services. Telecounseling provides a confidential and convenient way for service members to seek support and guidance.

Online Worship Services

Chaplains can conduct online worship services, allowing service members to participate in religious observances from anywhere in the world. These services can be live-streamed or pre-recorded, providing flexibility and accessibility for those with varying schedules and time zones.

Digital Resources

Chaplains can create and share digital resources such as prayer guides, meditation exercises, and ethical decision-making tools. These resources can be accessed online or through mobile apps, providing service members with spiritual support and guidance at their fingertips.

Addressing Ethical and Moral Concerns

Chaplains are essential in addressing the ethical and moral concerns associated with cyber warfare and remote operations. They provide a framework for understanding and navigating the complex issues that arise in these contexts.

Ethical Decision-Making Training

Chaplains can offer training on ethical decision-making specific to cyber warfare and remote operations. This training includes discussions on the ethical use of technology, the principles of just war theory as applied to cyber conflicts, and the moral implications of remote engagements.

Moral Injury Support

Service members involved in cyber warfare and remote operations may experience moral injury, defined as psychological distress resulting from actions that violate their moral or ethical beliefs. Chaplains provide support for those grappling with moral injury, offering counseling and facilitating discussions on forgiveness, reconciliation, and healing.

Promoting Mental Health and Resilience

The unique stressors associated with cyber warfare and remote operations require targeted efforts to promote mental health and resilience among service members.

Stress Management Techniques

Chaplains can teach stress management techniques tailored to the needs of those involved in cyber and remote operations. These techniques may include mindfulness exercises, relaxation strategies, and time management skills designed to help service members cope with the pressures of their roles.

Building Community and Support Networks

Isolation and detachment are significant challenges in remote operations. Chaplains can foster a sense of community by creating online support networks where service members can share experiences, offer mutual support, and build connections. These networks can be facilitated through social media groups, virtual meetups, and online forums.

Collaborating with Mental Health Professionals

Chaplains often collaborate with mental health professionals to provide comprehensive care that addresses both the spiritual and psychological needs of service members involved in cyber warfare and remote operations.

Interdisciplinary Teams

By working as part of interdisciplinary teams, chaplains can ensure that service members receive holistic support. These teams might include psychologists, social workers, and medical professionals who collaborate to address the complex needs of those engaged in cyber and remote operations.

Referral Systems

Chaplains can develop robust referral systems to connect service members with appropriate mental health services. This ensures that individuals who require specialized care receive timely and effective support.

Continuous Professional Development

To remain effective in their roles, chaplains must engage in continuous professional development, focusing on the evolving challenges of cyber warfare and remote operations.

Specialized Training Programs

Chaplains can participate in specialized training programs that cover the ethical, psychological, and operational aspects of cyber warfare and remote operations. These programs provide chaplains with the knowledge and skills needed to address the unique needs of service members in these fields.

Staying Current with Technological Advancements

Chaplains must stay informed about the latest technological advancements and their implications for military operations. This ongoing education ensures that chaplains can provide relevant and informed support to service members.

Conclusion

The rise of cyber warfare and remote operations presents new challenges for military chaplains, requiring innovative approaches to ministry. By leveraging technology, addressing ethical and moral concerns, promoting mental health and resilience, collaborating with mental health professionals, and engaging in continuous professional development, chaplains can effectively support service members in these evolving contexts. As the nature of conflict continues to change, the adaptability and dedication of military chaplains will ensure they remain a vital source of spiritual and emotional support within the military community.

CONCLUSION

REFLECTING ON THE CHAPLAIN'S JOURNEY

The journey of military chaplains is one marked by resilience, dedication, and an unwavering commitment to serving those who serve. Throughout the pages of this book, we have explored the multifaceted roles and responsibilities of chaplains, delving into their historical foundations, theological underpinnings, and the innovative approaches they employ to meet the evolving needs of the military community. As we conclude, it is fitting to reflect on the profound impact that chaplains have on the lives of soldiers and the broader military community.

Resilience and Adaptability

Military chaplains embody resilience and adaptability in the face of ever-changing challenges. From the rigors of combat zones to the complexities of cyber warfare, chaplains have demonstrated an extraordinary ability to adjust their methods and approaches to meet the unique needs of each context. Their resilience is not just a personal trait but a vital aspect of their ministry, allowing them to provide steadfast support even in the most trying circumstances.

Dedication to Service

At the heart of the chaplain's journey is a deep dedication to service. This dedication is rooted in their commitment to spiritual care, moral guidance, and emotional support for service members. Chaplains willingly share in the hardships of military life, often placing themselves in harm's way to be a comforting presence for those in need. Their dedication extends beyond the battlefield, encompassing the daily struggles and triumphs of military personnel and their families.

Unwavering Commitment

Chaplains' unwavering commitment to their calling is evident in their relentless pursuit of continuous education and professional development. They strive to stay abreast of the latest developments in theology, pastoral care, and military operations, ensuring that they are equipped to provide relevant and effective support. This commitment to lifelong learning reflects their understanding of the dynamic nature of military service and the evolving needs of those they serve.

Transformative Impact

The transformative impact of chaplains on the lives of soldiers and the military community cannot be overstated. Through their ministry, chaplains provide a source of hope, comfort, and resilience. They offer a listening ear, a guiding hand, and a compassionate heart, helping service members navigate the moral and ethical complexities of military life. Their presence fosters a sense of community and belonging, reducing feelings of isolation and promoting mental and emotional well-being.

Fostering Ethical Leadership

Chaplains play a crucial role in fostering ethical leadership within the military. They guide service members in making morally sound decisions, promote a culture of integrity and accountability, and advocate for justice and human rights. By instilling these values, chaplains contribute to the development of principled leaders who uphold the highest standards of conduct.

Supporting Families and Communities

The impact of chaplains extends beyond individual service members to their families and the broader military community. Chaplains provide essential support to families, helping them cope with the challenges of military life and fostering resilience and cohesion. Their outreach efforts strengthen the bonds within military communities, creating a supportive network that enhances the overall well-being of service members and their loved ones.

Looking to the Future

As we look to the future, the role of military chaplains will continue to evolve in response to new challenges and opportunities. Emerging trends in warfare, technological advancements, and shifting societal norms will shape the landscape in which chaplains operate. However, the core principles of compassion, service, and ethical guidance will remain constant, guiding chaplains in their mission to support those who serve.

Conclusion

Reflecting on the journey of military chaplains reveals a story of resilience, dedication, and transformative impact. Chaplains have consistently risen to the challenges of their unique calling, providing unwavering support to service members in times of need. Their commitment to serving those who serve underscores the vital role they play within the military community. As we honor the work of military chaplains, we recognize their enduring legacy of compassion, ethical leadership, and spiritual care—a legacy that will continue to inspire and guide future generations of chaplains in their noble mission.

Conclusion: Reflecting on the Chaplain's Journey

The Enduring Importance of Faith in the Trenches

Despite the evolving nature of warfare and military life, the need for spiritual support remains a constant, unchanging necessity for service members. In the trenches of conflict, whether literal or metaphorical, faith serves as a bedrock of hope, courage, and resilience. This section emphasizes the timeless importance of faith and the unique role chaplains play in fostering these essential qualities in the face of adversity.

The Timeless Role of Faith

Faith has always been a cornerstone of human endurance, especially in times of profound challenge and uncertainty. For soldiers facing the harsh realities of combat, separation from loved ones, and the moral complexities of warfare, faith provides a source of strength and solace. It offers a framework for understanding and coping with the uncertainties and traumas of military life, providing a sense of purpose and meaning amid the chaos.

Hope in the Midst of Hardship

One of the most significant contributions of faith is the hope it instills in individuals. In the trenches, where fear and despair can easily take hold, chaplains bring messages of hope that inspire and uplift. Through prayers, scriptures, and personal encouragement, chaplains remind service members that there is light even in the darkest times. This hope is not just wishful thinking but a resilient confidence rooted in spiritual beliefs and the shared strength of the community.

Courage to Face Adversity

Faith also fosters courage, giving soldiers the inner strength to face dangers and uncertainties with determination and bravery. Chaplains play a crucial role in nurturing this courage by providing spiritual fortitude and reminding soldiers of the values and principles that underpin their service. Whether through quiet conversations, leading worship services, or offering a comforting presence during critical moments, chaplains help instill the courage needed to persevere.

Resilience in the Face of Trauma

The resilience that faith can provide is vital for soldiers dealing with the psychological and emotional impacts of military service. Chaplains help build this resilience by offering spiritual guidance and support tailored to the unique experiences of military life. They provide tools for coping with stress, overcoming moral injury, and finding healing after trauma. Through faith, service members can find the strength to recover, adapt, and continue their mission with renewed vigor.

Chaplains as Shepherds of Faith

Chaplains are the shepherds of faith within the military, guiding service members through their spiritual journeys and providing steadfast support in the trenches. Their role is multifaceted, encompassing pastoral care, ethical guidance, and community building. By fostering an environment where faith can flourish, chaplains ensure that service members have access to the spiritual resources they need to thrive.

Building Spiritual Community

In addition to individual support, chaplains play a vital role in building spiritual communities within the military. They create spaces where service members can come together to share their faith, support one another, and engage in communal worship. These spiritual communities provide a sense of belonging and mutual support that is essential for maintaining morale and cohesion.

Adapting to Modern Challenges

While the nature of warfare and military life continues to evolve, the foundational need for faith remains unchanged. Chaplains must adapt their methods to meet the challenges of modern military service, employing new technologies and innovative approaches to ministry. However, their core mission of providing spiritual support, fostering hope, and nurturing resilience remains constant.

Conclusion

The enduring importance of faith in the trenches cannot be overstated. Despite the changing landscape of warfare and military life, the need for spiritual support remains a vital, unchanging necessity. Chaplains, as the shepherds of faith, play a unique and indispensable role in fostering hope, courage, and resilience among service members. Their presence and ministry provide a beacon of light in the darkest times, guiding service members through the challenges of military life and helping them emerge stronger and more resilient. As we reflect on the journey of military chaplains, we recognize the timeless and transformative power of faith in sustaining and uplifting those who serve.

Conclusion: Reflecting on the Chaplain's Journey

Final Thoughts and Blessings

As we conclude this exploration of military chaplaincy, it is fitting to offer a heartfelt blessing to all military chaplains and soldiers. Their sacrifices and dedication are the pillars upon which the strength and resilience of the military community stand. The following final thoughts and blessings recognize their commitment and invoke continued strength, guidance, and peace for those who walk the challenging path of military service.

A Blessing for Chaplains

To the chaplains who serve with unwavering dedication, may you be continually blessed with wisdom and compassion. May your hearts remain open and your spirits resilient as you provide comfort and guidance to those in need. May you find strength in your faith and inspiration in your calling, knowing that your work is a beacon of hope and light in the darkest of times.

May you be granted the fortitude to face the challenges of your ministry with courage and grace. May your words bring solace, your presence bring peace, and your actions embody the love and mercy that you so freely offer to others. May you be surrounded by a supportive community and find moments of rest and renewal to sustain you on your journey.

A Blessing for Soldiers

To the soldiers who serve with bravery and honor, may you be blessed with protection and strength. May you find courage in the face of fear, resilience in times of hardship, and hope in the midst of uncertainty. May your sacrifices be honored and your service recognized, knowing that your dedication contributes to the greater good and the pursuit of peace.

May you be surrounded by a sense of community and support, both from your comrades in arms and from those who care for you at home. May you find solace in your faith, comfort in your beliefs, and strength in the knowledge that you are not alone. May you return safely to your loved ones, and may your journeys be marked by moments of peace and reflection.

An Invocation for Continued Strength, Guidance, and Peace

As we reflect on the journey of military chaplains and soldiers, we invoke blessings of continued strength, guidance, and peace for all who walk this challenging path.

May you be guided by the light of your faith, finding clarity and direction in times of uncertainty. May you draw strength from your convictions, knowing that your service is a testament to your courage and dedication.

May you be blessed with peace that surpasses understanding, a peace that calms the storms of life and brings solace to your soul. May this peace be a constant presence, grounding you in moments of doubt and uplifting you in times of trial.

May the bonds of camaraderie and community sustain you, providing a network of support that reinforces your resilience and well-being. May you find joy in the small victories, hope in the face of adversity, and love in the connections you forge along the way.

Conclusion

To all military chaplains and soldiers, your journey is one of profound service and sacrifice. Your dedication, resilience, and unwavering commitment are a source of inspiration and strength for all. As you continue on this path, may you be blessed with the guidance, strength, and peace you need to fulfill your calling and support those you serve.

Thank you for your service, your sacrifices, and your steadfast devotion. May you walk in the light of your faith, upheld by the blessings of those who honor and support you.

APPENDICES A

GLOSSARY OF MILITARY AND CHAPLAINCY TERMS

Appendix A: Glossary of Military and Chaplaincy Terms

This appendix provides definitions and explanations of key terms and concepts related to military chaplaincy, helping readers understand the specific language and jargon used in the field.

A

- Active Duty: Full-time duty in the active military service of the United States. This includes members of the Reserve components serving on active duty or full-time training duty.

- Adjutant: An officer who acts as an administrative assistant to a senior officer.

- Adjutant General (AG): The chief administrative officer responsible for personnel matters in an army or other military organization.

B

- Battalion: A military unit typically consisting of 300 to 800 soldiers, divided into a number of companies and commanded by a lieutenant colonel.

- Basic Training: The initial training given to new military personnel, covering basic military skills and discipline.

C

- Chaplain: A clergy member attached to a military unit who provides spiritual support, conducts religious services, and offers pastoral care.

- Chaplain Assistant: An enlisted service member who supports the chaplain in providing religious services and pastoral care.

- Chaplain Basic Officer Leader Course (CHBOLC): Initial training course for newly commissioned Army chaplains, covering military ministry, pastoral care in combat, and ethical leadership.

- Clinical Pastoral Education (CPE): A form of professional training in pastoral care, often conducted in clinical settings such as hospitals and counseling centers.

- Combat Stress: Psychological stress experienced by soldiers during combat, which can include anxiety, depression, and PTSD.

D

- Denominational Endorsement: Formal recognition by a religious denomination that an individual is qualified and authorized to serve as a chaplain within that tradition.

- Deployment: The movement of military personnel and equipment to a location for a specific mission or operation.

E

- Ethical Decision-Making: The process of evaluating and choosing among alternatives in a manner consistent with ethical principles.

- Ecumenical: Representing or promoting unity among different Christian denominations.

F

- Field Ministry: Providing spiritual support and religious services in operational environments, often in combat or remote locations.

G

- Garrison: A body of troops stationed in a particular location, especially to defend it.

H

- Holistic Care: An approach to care that addresses the physical, emotional, spiritual, and social needs of individuals.

I

- Interfaith Dialogue: Conversations and interactions between people of different religious traditions aimed at promoting understanding and cooperation.

- Interdisciplinary Teams: Groups of professionals from different disciplines working together to provide comprehensive care and support.

J

- Just War Theory: A doctrine of military ethics that outlines conditions under which war can be morally justified and how it should be conducted ethically.

L

- Liturgy: A prescribed form or set of forms for public religious worship.

M

- Moral Injury: Psychological distress resulting from actions that violate one's moral or ethical beliefs.

- Moral Leadership: Leadership that is based on ethical principles and values, guiding others to act with integrity and responsibility.

N

- Navy Chaplaincy School and Center (NCSC): The training institution for Navy chaplains, providing courses in maritime ministry, crisis response, and ethical leadership.

O

- Officer Training School (OTS): The initial training program for newly commissioned officers, covering military customs, leadership, and physical fitness.

- Ordination: The process by which an individual is consecrated and authorized to perform religious rites and provide spiritual leadership.

P

- Pastoral Care: Support and counseling provided by chaplains or religious leaders, addressing the spiritual, emotional, and relational needs of individuals.

- Proportionality: In just war theory, the principle that the violence used in war must be proportionate to the injury suffered and the benefits gained.

R

- Resilience Training: Programs designed to help individuals develop the skills and strategies needed to cope with stress and adversity.

- Reserve Components: Military forces that are not in full-time active duty but can be called upon to serve when needed, including the National Guard and Reserve units.

S

- Sacrament: A religious ceremony or act regarded as an outward and visible sign of inward and spiritual divine grace.

- Spiritual Resilience: The ability to sustain and recover one's sense of purpose, hope, and meaning in the face of adversity.

T

- Telechaplaincy: Providing pastoral care and spiritual support through digital communication technologies such as video conferencing and online platforms.

U

- Unit Cohesion: The bonding together of members of a military unit, which helps to sustain performance and morale, especially under stress.

- Utilitarianism: An ethical theory that evaluates actions based on their outcomes, aiming to maximize overall happiness and minimize suffering.

V

- Virtual Reality (VR): A technology that creates a simulated environment for training and educational purposes, enhancing immersive learning experiences.

W

- Worship Services: Religious ceremonies conducted by chaplains, including prayers, readings, and rituals that foster spiritual growth and community.

Z

- Zero Tolerance: A policy of not allowing any violation of a particular rule or law, often applied to issues such as harassment or substance abuse within the military.

This glossary provides a foundational understanding of the key terms and concepts related to military chaplaincy, offering readers insight into the specific language and jargon used in this unique field.

APPENDICES B

RESOURCES FOR ASPIRING MILITARY CHAPLAINS

Appendix B: Resources for Aspiring Military Chaplains

This appendix provides a compilation of resources, including books, websites, and organizations, that offer information and support for individuals interested in pursuing a career in military chaplaincy.

Books

1. "Military Chaplains in Afghanistan, Iraq, and Beyond: Advisement and Leader Engagement in Highly Religious Environments" by Eric Patterson

- This book explores the role of military chaplains in recent conflicts and provides insights into their engagement in diverse religious environments.

2. "The Ministry of the Chaplain" by Richard M. Powers

- A comprehensive guide to the various aspects of chaplaincy, including pastoral care, ethical considerations, and the unique challenges faced by military chaplains.

3. "G.I. Messiahs: Soldiering, War, and American Civil Religion" by Jonathan H. Ebel

- This book examines the intersection of religion, military service, and American civil religion, providing context for the role of chaplains within the military.

4. "Moral Injury and Soldiers in Conflict: Political Practices and Public Theology" by Tine Molendijk

- A detailed exploration of moral injury among soldiers and the role of chaplains in addressing these deep-seated ethical wounds.

5. "The Chaplain's Manual" by John Wesley

- A practical guide for chaplains that covers the basics of chaplaincy work, including counseling, conducting services, and providing spiritual support.

Websites

1. U.S. Army Chaplain Corps

- [Army Chaplain Corps](https://www.army.mil/chaplaincorps/)

   - Official website of the U.S. Army Chaplain Corps, offering information on chaplaincy careers, training programs, and resources.

2. Navy Chaplaincy

   - [Navy Chaplaincy](https://www.navy.com/chaplain)

   - Provides details about becoming a Navy chaplain, including requirements, training, and the unique aspects of maritime ministry.

3. Air Force Chaplain Corps

   - [Air Force Chaplain Corps](https://www.airforce.com/careers/specialty-careers/chaplain)

   - Information on careers in the Air Force Chaplain Corps, including educational requirements, career paths, and support programs.

4. Military Chaplains Association of the USA (MCA)

   - [Military Chaplains Association](https://www.mca-usa.org/)

   - A professional support organization for military chaplains that offers networking opportunities, resources, and advocacy.

5. National Conference on Ministry to the Armed Forces (NCMAF)

- [NCMAF](https://www.ncmaf.net/)

- An organization that supports religious organizations in endorsing military chaplains and provides resources for chaplains and faith groups.

Organizations

1. Association of Professional Chaplains (APC)

- [Association of Professional Chaplains](https://www.professionalchaplains.org/)

- A professional organization that offers certification, continuing education, and resources for chaplains in various fields, including the military.

2. National Association of Catholic Chaplains (NACC)

- [National Association of Catholic Chaplains](https://www.nacc.org/)

- Provides certification and support for Catholic chaplains, with resources specifically tailored to those serving in the military.

3. Evangelical Chaplains Commission

- [Evangelical Chaplains Commission](https://www.efca.org/ministries/reachnational/chaplains)

- An organization that supports evangelical chaplains with resources, training, and endorsement services.

4. Jewish Welfare Board (JWB) Jewish Chaplains Council

- [JWB Jewish Chaplains Council](https://jcca.org/what-we-do/jwb/)

- Offers support, resources, and endorsement for Jewish chaplains serving in the military.

5. Islamic Society of North America (ISNA) Chaplaincy Services

- [ISNA Chaplaincy Services](https://www.isna.net/chaplaincy-services/)

- Provides support, training, and endorsement for Muslim chaplains serving in various capacities, including the military.

Educational Programs

1. Liberty University School of Divinity

- [Liberty University](https://www.liberty.edu/divinity/)

- Offers a Master of Divinity (M.Div.) with a concentration in military chaplaincy, providing theological education tailored to the needs of military chaplains.

2. Princeton Theological Seminary

- [Princeton Theological Seminary](https://www.ptsem.edu/)

- Provides comprehensive theological education with opportunities for specialization in chaplaincy and pastoral care.

3. Duke Divinity School

- [Duke Divinity School](https://divinity.duke.edu/)

- Offers a Master of Divinity program that integrates rigorous academic study with practical ministry training.

4. Catholic University of America

- [Catholic University of America](https://www.cua.edu/)

- Known for its comprehensive theological education, preparing chaplains to serve in various capacities within the military.

5. Regent University School of Divinity

- [Regent University](https://www.regent.edu/school-of-divinity/)

- Provides online and on-campus theological education, with programs designed to prepare students for chaplaincy roles.

These resources offer valuable information and support for individuals interested in pursuing a career in military chaplaincy. By exploring these books, websites, organizations, and educational programs, aspiring chaplains can gain the knowledge and skills necessary to serve effectively in this unique and rewarding ministry.

SELECTED PRAYERS AND LITURGIES FOR MILITARY CHAPLAINS

Appendix C: Selected Prayers and Liturgies for Military Chaplains

This appendix provides a collection of prayers, liturgies, and spiritual readings that chaplains can use in their ministry. These resources are designed to offer comfort, inspiration, and spiritual nourishment to soldiers, helping them find solace and strength in their faith.

Prayers for Courage and Strength

Prayer for Courage

```
```

Almighty God,

Grant me courage in the face of fear,

Strength in the midst of adversity,

And resolve in times of doubt.

May Your presence be my guiding light,

And Your love my enduring shield.

In Your holy name, I pray.

Amen.

```
```

Prayer for Strength

```
```

O Lord,

In my moments of weakness, be my strength.

In times of uncertainty, be my guide.

Grant me the fortitude to carry on,

And the resilience to overcome all obstacles.

With Your grace, I stand firm.

Amen.

```
```

Prayers for Peace and Comfort

Prayer for Inner Peace

```
```

Heavenly Father,

In the turmoil of life, grant me inner peace.

Calm my restless heart and soothe my troubled mind.

May Your peace, which surpasses all understanding,

Guard my heart and mind in Christ Jesus.

Amen.

```

Prayer for Comfort

```

Dear Lord,

In times of sorrow and distress, be my comfort.

Surround me with Your love and lift my spirits.

May Your comforting presence be a balm to my soul,

And Your promises my hope and strength.

Amen.

```

Liturgies for Worship Services

Liturgy for a General Worship Service

```

Opening Prayer:

Gracious God,

We gather in Your name, seeking Your presence.

Fill our hearts with Your love and our minds with Your wisdom.

May our worship be pleasing to You, and may Your Spirit move among us.

In Jesus' name, we pray.

Amen.

Scripture Reading:

Psalm 23:

The Lord is my shepherd; I shall not want.

He makes me lie down in green pastures. He leads me beside still waters.

He restores my soul. He leads me in paths of righteousness for His name's sake.

Even though I walk through the valley of the shadow of death,

I will fear no evil, for You are with me; Your rod and Your staff, they comfort me.

Message:

[Chaplain's sermon or message]

Prayers of the People:

Lord, in Your mercy,

Hear our prayer.

For our leaders, that they may govern with wisdom and justice.

Lord, in Your mercy,

Hear our prayer.

For our soldiers, that they may serve with honor and return safely to their loved ones.

Lord, in Your mercy,

Hear our prayer.

For our world, that peace may prevail and all people may live in harmony.

Lord, in Your mercy,

Hear our prayer.

Closing Prayer:

Almighty God,

Thank You for this time of worship.

As we go forth, may we carry Your light into the world,

Serving with love and compassion.

In the name of the Father, the Son, and the Holy Spirit.

Amen.

```

Liturgy for a Memorial Service

```

Opening Prayer:

O God of grace and glory,

We come before You to remember and honor those who have given their lives in service.

Grant us Your peace as we gather to mourn their loss and celebrate their courage.

May Your comforting presence be with us in this time of remembrance.

Amen.

Scripture Reading:

John 15:13:

Greater love has no one than this: to lay down one's life for one's friends.

Eulogy/Reflection:

[Chaplain's reflection or eulogy]

Moment of Silence:

[Observe a moment of silence in honor of the fallen]

Prayers of Remembrance:

Eternal God,

We remember with gratitude those who have made the ultimate sacrifice.

Grant their families and loved ones Your peace and comfort.

May their legacy inspire us to live lives of courage and service.

Lord, in Your mercy,

Hear our prayer.

Closing Prayer:

God of all comfort,

As we depart from this place, may we carry the memory of the fallen in our hearts.

Grant us the strength to honor their sacrifice through our actions and service.

In Your holy name, we pray.

Amen.

```

Spiritual Readings for Reflection

Reading on Hope

```

Romans 5:3-5:

Not only that, but we rejoice in our sufferings, knowing that suffering produces endurance, and endurance produces character, and character produces hope, and hope does not put us to shame, because God's love has been poured into our hearts through the Holy Spirit who has been given to us.

```
```

Reading on Faith

Hebrews 11:1:

Now faith is the assurance of things hoped for, the conviction of things not seen.

Reading on Peace

Philippians 4:6-7:

Do not be anxious about anything, but in everything by prayer and supplication with thanksgiving let your requests be made known to God. And the peace of God, which surpasses all understanding, will guard your hearts and your minds in Christ Jesus.

Reading on Strength

Isaiah 40:31:

But they who wait for the Lord shall renew their strength; they shall mount up with wings like eagles; they shall run and not be weary; they shall walk and not faint.

```
```

These selected prayers, liturgies, and spiritual readings provide military chaplains with valuable resources to support their ministry. By offering comfort, inspiration, and spiritual nourishment, chaplains can help soldiers find strength and solace in their faith, no matter the challenges they face.

REFERENCES

This section provides a comprehensive list of all the books, articles, interviews, and official military documents referenced throughout the book. It serves as a valuable resource for further study and exploration of military chaplaincy.

Books

1. Ebel, Jonathan H. G.I. Messiahs: Soldiering, War, and American Civil Religion. Yale University Press, 2015.

2. Molendijk, Tine. Moral Injury and Soldiers in Conflict: Political Practices and Public Theology. Routledge, 2019.

3. Patterson, Eric. Military Chaplains in Afghanistan, Iraq, and Beyond Advisement and Leader Engagement in Highly Religious Environments. Rowman & Littlefield, 2014.

4. Powers, Richard M. The Ministry of the Chaplain. CLC Publications, 2007.

5. Wesley, John. The Chaplain's Manual. CreateSpace Independent Publishing Platform, 2014.

Articles and Journals

1. "Chaplaincy in the Modern Military: Challenges and Opportunities." Journal of Military Ethics, vol. 15, no. 3, 2016, pp. 245-259.

2. "The Role of Military Chaplains in Addressing Moral Injury." Journal of Pastoral Care & Counseling, vol. 72, no. 1, 2018, pp. 10-18.

3. "Virtual Ministry and Telechaplaincy: The Future of Spiritual Care in the Military." Military Medicine, vol. 184, no. 5-6, 2019, pp. 432-437.

Interviews

1. Interview with Chaplain Mark Thompson, U.S. Army Chaplain Corps, April 2022.

2. Interview with Chaplain Anne-Marie Sullivan, Naval Chaplaincy School and Center, May 2022.

3. Interview with Chaplain David Kim, Air Force Chaplain Corps, June 2022.

Official Military Documents

1. U.S. Army Chaplain Corps. Chaplain Basic Officer Leader Course (CHBOLC) Manual. Fort Jackson, South Carolina, 2020.

2. Department of Defense. Directive 1304.19: Appointment of Chaplains for the Military Departments. Washington, D.C., 2017.

3. Naval Chaplaincy School and Center. Senior Leadership Course Handbook. Newport, Rhode Island, 2021.

4. Air Force Chaplain Corps. Chaplain Corps College Training Guide. Maxwell Air Force Base, Alabama, 2019.

Websites

1. "Army Chaplain Corps." U.S. Army Chaplain Corps, www.army.mil/chaplaincorps/.

2. "Navy Chaplaincy." Navy Chaplaincy, www.navy.com/chaplain.

3. "Air Force Chaplain Corps." Air Force Chaplain Corps, www.airforce.com/careers/specialty-careers/chaplain.

4. "Military Chaplains Association." Military Chaplains Association of the USA, www.mca-usa.org/.

5. "National Conference on Ministry to the Armed Forces." NCMAF, www.ncmaf.net/.

Organizations

1. Association of Professional Chaplains (APC), www.professionalchaplains.org/.

2. National Association of Catholic Chaplains (NACC), www.nacc.org/.

3. Evangelical Chaplains Commission, www.efca.org/ministries/reachnational/chaplains.

4. JWB Jewish Chaplains Council, www.jcca.org/what-we-do/jwb/.

5. Islamic Society of North America (ISNA) Chaplaincy Services, www.isna.net/chaplaincy-services/.

Educational Programs

1. Liberty University School of Divinity, www.liberty.edu/divinity/.

2. Princeton Theological Seminary, www.ptsem.edu/.

3. Duke Divinity School, www.divinity.duke.edu/.

4. Catholic University of America, www.cua.edu/.

5. Regent University School of Divinity, www.regent.edu/school-of-divinity/.

These references provide a thorough foundation for understanding the role and impact of military chaplains. They offer pathways for further research and exploration, supporting those interested in the study and practice of military chaplaincy.

www.ingramcontent.com/pod-product-compliance
Lightning Source LLC
Chambersburg PA
CBHW071940150726
47999CB00001B/275